Study Guide

Criminal Law

NINTH EDITION

Joel Samaha
University of Minnesota

Prepared by

Lore Rutz-Burri
Southern Oregon University

Australia • Brazil • Canada • Mexico • Singapore • Spain • United Kingdom • United States

© 2008 Thomson Wadsworth, a part of The Thomson Corporation. Thomson, the Star logo, and Wadsworth are trademarks used herein under license.

ALL RIGHTS RESERVED. No part of this work covered by the copyright hereon may be reproduced or used in any form or by any means—graphic, electronic, or mechanical, including photocopying, recording, taping, Web distribution, information storage and retrieval systems, or in any other manner—without the written permission of the publisher.

Printed in the United States of America

1 2 3 4 5 6 7 11 10 09 08 07

Printer: West

ISBN-13: 978-0-495-38401-4
ISBN-10: 0-495-38401-1

Thomson Higher Education
10 Davis Drive
Belmont, CA 94002-3098
USA

For more information about our products, contact us at:
Thomson Learning Academic Resource Center
1-800-423-0563

For permission to use material from this text or product, submit a request online at
http://www.thomsonrights.com.
Any additional questions about permissions can be submitted by email to
thomsonrights@thomson.com.

TABLE OF CONTENTS

STUDY GUIDE

1 THE NATURE AND LIMITS OF CRIMINAL LAW IN U.S. SOCIETY — 1

2 CONSTITUTIONAL LIMITATIONS ON CRIMINAL LAW — 20

3 THE GENERAL PRINCIPLES OF CRIMINAL LIABILITY: *ACTUS REUS* — 38

4 THE GENERAL PRINCIPLES OF CRIMINAL LIABILITY: *MENS REA*, CONCURRENCE, AND CAUSATION — 54

5 DEFENSES TO CRIMINAL LIABILITY: JUSTIFICATIONS — 70

6 DEFENSES TO CRIMINAL LIABILITY: EXCUSES — 86

7 PARTIES TO CRIME AND VICARIOUS LIABILITY — 103

8 INCHOATE CRIMES: ATTEMPT, CONSPIRACY, AND SOLICITATION — 118

9 CRIMES AGAINST PERSONS I: HOMICIDE — 136

10 CRIMES AGAINST PERSONS II: CRIMINAL SEXUAL CONDUCT, BODILY INJURY, AND PERSONAL RESTRAINT — 156

11 CRIMES AGAINST PROPERTY — 178

12 CRIMES AGAINST PUBLIC ORDER AND MORALS — 196

13 CRIMES AGAINST THE STATE — 214

CHAPTER 1
THE NATURE AND LIMITS OF CRIMINAL LAW IN U.S. SOCIETY

LEARNING OBJECTIVES

After studying this chapter, students will understand that:

- Criminal law is about blaming and punishing people for crimes.

- Criminal law is only *one* kind of social control.

- The *most* important difference between torts and crimes is the conviction, which expresses the community's hatred of, fear of, or contempt for the convict.

- Classifying crimes reflects the urge to make sense of criminal law.

- Criminal law consists of a general part which includes principles that apply to more than one crime, and a special part which defines the elements of specific crimes.

- The purposes of punishment include retribution which looks back to punish past criminal conduct, and prevention which looks ahead to prevent future criminal conduct.

- Law, not individuals, controls government power.

- Judges are restrained in their lawmaking power by the rule of lenity, precedent, and *stare decisis*.

- The sources of criminal law in our federal system can be found mostly in state criminal codes and municipal codes.

- There is a substantial and growing body of criminal law in the U.S. Criminal Code and in administrative agencies.

- The common denominator in U.S. criminal law is the Model Penal Code.

KEY TERMS AND CONCEPTS

- **torts**—private wrongs for which you can sue the party who wronged you and recover money; p. 8

- **plaintiffs**—those who sue for wrongs in tort cases; p. 8

- **damages**—money plaintiffs get for the injuries they suffer; p. 8

- **punitive damages**—damages that make an example of defendants and punish them for their behavior; p. 10

- **felonies**—serious crimes that are generally punishable by one year or more in prison; p. 10

- **misdemeanors**—minor crimes for which the penalty is usually less than one year in jail or a fine; p. 10

- *malum in se*—a crime inherently bad or evil; p. 11

- *malum prohibitum*—a crime not inherently bad or evil but merely prohibited; p. 11

- **general part of criminal law**—principles that apply to all crimes; p. 12

- **special part of criminal law**—defines the elements of specific crimes; p. 12

- **complicity**—the principle regarding parties to crime that establishes the conditions under which more than one person incurs liability before, during, and after committing crimes; when one person is liable for another person's crime; p. 13

- **liability**—the technical legal term for responsibility; p. 13

- **criminal punishment**—punishments prescribed by legislatures; p. 13

- **retribution**—punishment based on just deserts; p. 14

- **prevention**—punishing offenders to prevent crimes in the future; p. 16

- **culpability**—blameworthiness based on *mens rea;* deserving of punishment because of individual responsibility for actions; p. 15

- **general deterrence (also called general prevention)**—aims, by threat of punishment, to deter criminal behavior in the general population; p. 16

- **special deterrence**—the threat of punishment aimed at individual offenders in the hope of deterring future criminal conduct; p. 16

- **incapacitation**—punishment by imprisonment, mutilation, and even death; p. 16

- **rehabilitation**—prevention of crime by treatment; p. 16

- **principle of utility**—permitting only the minimum amount of pain necessary to prevent the crime as punishment; p. 16

- **principle of legality**—a principle stating that there can be no crime or punishment if there are no specific laws forewarning citizens that certain specific conduct will result in a particular punishment; p. 20

- **retroactive criminal lawmaking**—people can't be convicted of, or punished for, a crime unless the law defined the crime and prescribed the punishment *before* they acted; "*the* first principle of criminal law;" p. 21

- **discretionary decision making**—judicial criminal lawmaking power that leaves judges lots of leeway for making decisions based on their professional training and experience; p. 23

- **rule of lenity**—when judges apply a criminal statute to a defendant, they have to stick "clearly within the letter of the statute," resolving all ambiguities in favor of the defendant and against the application of the statute; p. 24

- **precedent**—a prior court decision that guides judges in deciding future cases; p. 25

- *stare decisis*—the principle that binds courts to stand by prior decisions and leave settled points of law undisturbed; p. 25

- **common-law crimes**—crimes originating in the English common law; p. 28

- **criminal codes**—definitions of crimes and punishments by elected legislatures; p. 29

- **code states**—states that have abolished the common law; p. 29

- **Model Penal Code**—the code developed by the American Law Institute to guide reform in criminal law; p. 32

- **administrative crimes**—violations of federal and state agency rules; p. 34

CHAPTER OUTLINE

I. Conduct that Unjustifiably Inflicts Harm
    A. This is the definition of criminal liability; not all wrongs are crimes.

II. Crimes and Non-criminal Wrongs
    A. Criminal law is one form of social control, but there are others.
    B. Torts are similar to crimes in that they are a set of rules which apply to everyone in the community, and the power of the law backs them up.
    C. Torts are dissimilar to crimes in that they are brought by nongovernmental parties called plaintiffs who can only get money damages.
    D. Unlike crimes, there is no conviction or public condemnation if the party is found responsible for the wrongdoing.

III. Classifying Crimes
    A. Response to an urge to make sense of criminal law
    B. Helps us to think critically about criminal law
    C. **Felony and Misdemeanor**—Classifications based on punishment
        1. Felonies—defined
        2. Misdemeanors—defined
        3. Distinction matters
            a. Element in another crime
            b. Procedures for felonies are different
            c. Prior felony convictions may enhance sentence
            d. Legal consequences of felonies (for example, voting rights) which aren't there for misdemeanors
    D. *Malum in se* and *Malum prohibitum*—inherently evil or not
        1. Definitions
        2. Moral overtones
        3. Examples of each
        4. Classification may have legal consequences (for example, deporting aliens or disbarring lawyers).

IV. The General and Special Parts of Criminal Law
    A. **The General Part**
        1. Broad propositions that apply to more than one crime
        2. Crimes of general applicability, such as attempt, conspiracy, solicitation
        3. Principles of complicity
        4. Principles of justifications and excuses
    B. **The Special Part**
        1. Defines specific crimes; spells out the elements of the crime
            a. Crimes against persons
            b. Crimes against property
            c. Crimes against public order and morals
            d. Crimes against the state

V. Criminal Punishment
A. Punishment takes many forms, but each must meet the four criteria (inflict pain, be prescribed by the law that defines the crime, be intentionally administered, and be administered by the state).
B. Distinguish between punishment and treatment—not always clear
C. **Retribution**—punishing individuals for their past crimes
   1. Retributionists assume that offenders choose behavior which makes their choice blameworthy, and they assume offenders have free will.
   2. Underpinnings of retribution: culpability and justice
   3. Problems with restitution: abstract notions of justice, how much is just desert; urge to retaliate isn't part of civilized society; free will debate; crimes without culpability requirement (for example, statutory rape)
D. **Prevention**
   1. Types of prevention
      a. General deterrence—arguments in support and against
      b. Special deterrence—arguments in support and against
      c. Incapacitation—arguments in support and against
      d. Rehabilitation—arguments in support and against
   2. Principle of utility—defined
E. **Trends in Punishment**
   1. Societies have justified punishment on grounds of the four types of prevention, but have emphasized one over the others during different times and eras.

VI. The Principle of Legality
A. Law controls the power of government.
B. Values of fairness, liberty, democracy, and equality

VII. "No Crime without Law; No Punishment without Law"
A. Principle of Legality is a ban on making behavior criminal after its occurrence (retroactive criminal lawmaking).
B. The first principle of criminal law
   1. A person can't be convicted of, or punished for, a crime unless the law was already written before he or she acted.
C. **Legislative Retroactive Criminal Lawmaking**
   1. Legislatures can't pass retroactive criminal statutes.
D. **Judicial Retroactive Criminal Lawmaking**
   1. Debate whether judges should be allowed to interpret statutes in such a way that it is tantamount to law making
   2. Even proponents want to use it sparingly, to serve justice
   3. Special role of judges as moderators of the criminal law
   4. Judges already have tremendous discretion and make decisions based on their training and experience.
   5. The rule of lenity, directing how judges will interpret the law, influences judges in their lawmaking as well.
   6. Precedent and *stare decisis* greatly influence judges' lawmaking powers.

VIII. The Sources of Criminal Law

A. In addition to legislative and judicial lawmaking, there are several sources of criminal law. Most current criminal law is created by state legislatures or local governing bodies. Federal Congress and administrative agencies are also responsible for much of the current criminal law.

B. **Common-law Crimes**—Law that emerged over a long period of time and was based on customs and traditions passed down. Many states have common law in their history, but most have now abolished it to some extent. There are no official federal common-law crimes; however, as judges interpret congressional acts and engage in judicial lawmaking, they are creating federal common law.

C. **State Criminal Codes**—Periodically, states have been urged to abolish common-law crimes and establish a criminal law based solely upon criminal codes (called the codification movement).

D. **The Model Penal Code (MPC)**—The American Law Institute, which took several decades to create, culminated a draft code in 1962 which abolished common-law crimes. Even states which have not strictly abolished their codes have been influenced by the MPC.

E. **Municipal Ordinances**—Municipalities have broad but not unlimited power to create local crime laws and determine the punishment for those crimes. Some of the limitations on this power includes constitutional limitations, the state's having a conflicting law, and the inability to create felonies or crimes for which the punishment is more than one year of jail time.

F. **Administrative Agency Crimes**—State and federal agencies also make administrative rules which have criminal penalties. The constitution may limit the agency's authority to create and punish these as crimes.

IX. Criminal Law in a Federal System

A. There are fifty-two criminal codes in America—one for each state, the District of Columbia, and the U.S. Criminal Code for the federal government.

B. These codes resemble one another but they differ significantly in both the definitions of crimes and the severity of punishment.

X. The Text-Case Method

A. Two parts of the book
1. The Text defines and explains concepts and principles.
2. The Case Excerpts test your understanding (and get you to think critically by applying definitions, concepts, and principles to real cases).

B. **The Parts of the Case Excerpts**
1. Each case has a title, a citation, a procedural history, the name of the judge who wrote the opinion, a section discussing the facts of the case, the court's decision or judgment, and the court's opinion. The court's (majority) opinion is made up of the court's holding and the court's reasoning — or why the court decided as it did.
    a. Majority opinions
    b. Concurring opinions
    c. Dissenting opinions

Chapter 1: The Nature and Limits of Criminal Law in U.S. Society

    C. **Briefing the Case Excerpts**—In briefing a case, the important things that you should note are the important facts of the case, the legal issue that the court had to address, how the court decided the issues and why (the reasoning—the justifications the court gave for deciding how it did).

    D. Summary of briefing cases—Not every case will have every part, so briefing cases gets easier with practice. Generally, briefs will always have a facts (what happened) section.

XI. Finding Cases

    A. The ability to locate a case depends on understanding the components of the case citation. A case citation includes the volume of the reporter, the page number upon which the case starts, and the year of the decision.

CHAPTER SUMMARY

Not all wrongs are crimes, and using the criminal law is only one mechanism of social control. Criminal law decides who is criminally liable for what crime and what the response to that crime should be. Alternately, torts are private wrongs for which a nongovernmental party sues the wrongdoer for monetary damages. Although torts are similar to crimes, and sometimes even have the same name as related crimes, they are treated differently and do not result in a conviction with societal condemnation.

Crimes can be classified or graded according to many schemes. The most common are felony or misdemeanor. Typically a crime is a felony if it is punishable by at least one year in a state prison. Misdemeanors are punishable by one year or less in a local jail. Some crimes cover behavior that is *malum in se*, which means bad in itself or inherently evil. Murder is an example of a *malum in se* crime. Other crimes cover behavior that is unlawful only because the law says it is. These are called *malum prohibitum* crimes. Crimes can also be classified according to the subject or the value that is harmed. Examples would be crimes against person, property, public order, public morals, and the administration of justice.

The criminal law itself can be divided into two parts: the special part of the criminal law provides the definitions of various crimes; and the general part provides general principles that apply to all offenses. This would include *mens rea* provisions and accomplice liability provisions. The specific part of criminal law is where the definitions of crimes are found.

Criminal law is guided by considerations of the purposes of criminal punishment. Punishment has two goals: retribution and prevention. Retribution is the idea of an eye for an eye. Criminals should be blamed and pay their debt to society. Preventing further crime is the second goal. There are four kinds of prevention: general deterrence—which punishes someone to make an example of him; special deterrence—which punishes offenders to prevent them from committing more crimes; incapacitation—which prevents criminals from committing more crimes by locking them up; and rehabilitation—which prevents future crimes by changing or treating the individual offender. Although every society has justified criminal punishment based upon retribution or the four types of prevention, the degree of emphasis has varied in different eras.

The government's ability to make criminal law is limited by the principle of legality (or rule of law). This principle indicates that criminal laws should value fairness, liberty, democracy, and equality. Legislators are forbidden from making laws that apply retroactively to behavior which has already occurred. Judges, however, are allowed to exercise their judgment (called discretionary decision making) in deciding cases, but they are bound by the U.S. and state constitutions, the rule of lenity (a rule concerning how to interpret statutes), precedent, and *stare decisis*.

Legislation is only one of several sources of criminal law. American criminal law is derived from English common law. Common law was judge-made law based on the common customs. Over time, English common law has been supplemented by statutes (or codes). Today, most criminal law is found in state codes and municipal codes. These codes have been greatly influenced by the Model Penal Code, which was completed in 1962. Nevertheless, judges continue to be a source of law by their interpretations of the constitution and statutes. Additionally, administrative agencies have been delegated the task of creating criminal laws and penalties.

The Constitution establishes a federal system for America. Power is shared and divided between the states and federal government. Thus, both the states and the federal government can pass criminal laws. We have fifty sets of state criminal law, the criminal law in the District of Columbia, and the criminal law of the federal government. Although there are some common basic concepts, there are many differences among these jurisdictions.

The textbook uses the text-case method. It includes explanatory text and excerpts from court cases/opinions. Generally, only appellate courts write opinions. The party who appeals is called the appellant. The party whose victory in the court below is being challenged is called the appellee.

When reading case opinions or excerpts, students need to be able to find the various parts of the cases. Only the majority opinion establishes law and the precedent. There may also be concurring opinions and dissenting opinions. These may provide well-reasoned alternatives to the majority opinion which may, at some later time, become the law of the land. Two of the most important parts of the case are the holding and the rationale. The holding is the legal rule announced by the court that decides the case. The rationale is the reasons underlying the holding.

Finally, students should be able to find court cases by using the opinion citation system. To do this, students need to know the components of a legal citation, including the name of the case, the volume, reporter, page, and year of publication. There are a wide variety of publications and reporters for different jurisdictions.

PRACTICE TEST BANK

MULTIPLE CHOICE

1. A tort is a _____.

    a. private wrong
    b. type of crime
    c. type of pastry
    d. specific monetary punishment

2. Which of the following is a correct statement about felonies and misdemeanors?

    a. Historically, the distinction between felonies and misdemeanors was important, but today there is no need for such a classification.
    b. The criminal procedure is the same for both felonies and misdemeanors.
    c. The legal consequences for felony convictions may last long after the punishment for the conviction.
    d. Misdemeanors are generally less serious or blameworthy crimes.

3. One primary distinction between a crime and a tort is _____.

    a. the tort is brought by a government official acting on behalf of the citizens of that jurisdiction
    b. the crime is brought by a government official acting on behalf of the citizens of that jurisdiction
    c. the individual found responsible for a tort can receive many forms of punishment including fines, incarceration, and community service
    d. crimes, but not torts, harm the community as a whole

4. An eye for an eye approach to punishment is consistent with _____.

    a. general deterrence
    b. special deterrence
    c. incapacitation
    d. retribution

5. Retribution logically requires that the criminal be _____.

    a. blameworthy or culpable
    b. capable of change and wanting to change
    c. a potential re-offender or threat to society
    d. predictably dangerous or potentially dangerous

6. The idea of _____ involves confinement, surgical alteration, or execution to prevent further crimes by that defendant.

    a. rehabilitation
    b. special deterrence
    c. incapacitation
    d. retribution

7. The part of the criminal law that provides the elements of various particular crimes is called the _____ part.

    a. specific
    b. special
    c. specious
    d. spurious

8. In most jurisdictions, a felony is defined as a crime that is punishable by incarceration of at least _____ year(s) in a prison.

    a. one
    b. two
    c. three
    d. five

9. Crimes such as murder and rape, which involve inherently evil conduct, are termed ____.

    a. *malum prohibitum*
    b. *malum in se*
    c. incorporatum
    d. excelsis

10. Which of the following statements is most accurate regarding the criminal law in the U.S.?

    a. There is very little variation between jurisdictions because all states have adopted most of the Model Penal Code.
    b. There is very little variation between jurisdictions because all jurisdictions must conform to the U.S. Constitution and the U.S. Supreme Court decision.
    c. For a number of reasons, there is significant variation among jurisdictions in the U.S.
    d. Because of the Eighth Amendment, there are some differences between jurisdictions.

11. Under the principle of federalism, government power is allocated between _____.

    a. state (and local) governments and the federal government
    b. the federal government and the United Nations
    c. state and local governments
    d. state government and the United Nations

12. In the U.S. today, most criminal law is _____ law.

    a. federal
    b. state
    c. county
    d. international

13. American criminal law has its origin in English _____.

    a. civil law
    b. Code law
    c. Common law
    d. Royal decrees

14. Today, at least half the states have _____.

    a. retained common-law crimes as their only crimes
    b. abolished common-law crimes
    c. recognized common-law, statutory, and international crimes
    d. abolished their penal/criminal/crime codes

15. A code state is one which has _____.

    a. retained common-law crimes as their only crimes
    b. abolished common-law crimes
    c. recognized common-law, statutory, and international crimes
    d. abolished their penal/criminal/crime codes

16. Most states and the federal government have _____ levels of appellate courts.

    a. two
    b. three
    c. four
    d. five

17. In a court case/opinion, the legal rule that decides the case is called the _____.

    a. issue
    b. holding
    c. judgment
    d. reasoning

18. The established law of the case and the precedent is established in the _____ opinion.

    a. dominant
    b. concurring
    c. majority
    d. plurality

19. In the citation, 428 U.S. 364 (1976), 428 represents _____.

    a. the volume number
    b. the reporter
    c. the page number upon which the case begins
    d. the number of pages the decision is

20. Administrative law is _____.

    a. judge-made law
    b. law enacted by legislators
    c. law enacted by municipalities
    d. agency-made law

21. Punitive damages are _____.

    a. monetary damages designed to punish a civil defendant
    b. punishment which includes incarceration
    c. monetary damages designed to make the civil plaintiff whole
    d. like restitution and help cover the cost of treatment for the plaintiff

22. The idea that judges should strictly interpret statutes is referred to as _____.

    a. the principle of legality
    b. the principle of lenity
    c. the first principle
    d. the principle of utility

23. Which of the following does NOT restrain judicial discretion?

    a. precedent
    b. discretionary decision making
    c. the U.S. and state constitutions
    d. the principle of lenity

24. The Model Penal Code was drafted by the _____.

    a. American Law Institute
    b. Center for Legal Codification
    c. American Bar Association
    d. Committee for Equal Justice under the Law

25. Ordinances are laws enacted by _____.

    a. state legislators
    b. Federal Congress
    c. municipalities
    d. judges through their case interpretations

26. Placing a tax on cigarettes in order to discourage cigarette smoking is an example of a _____.

    a. crime
    b. non-criminal wrong
    c. license
    d. regulation

27. Conduct that unjustifiably and inexcusably inflicts or threatens harm to an individual or public interest is the definition of _____.

    a. a tort
    b. a contract
    c. criminal liability
    d. a regulation

28. Hunting without a license is an example of a _____ crime.

    a. *mala in se*
    b. regulation
    c. *mala prohibitum*
    d. general

Study Guide

29. Which of the following is the best example of criminal punishment?

   a. a mental patient confined indefinitely to a padded cell in a state hospital
   b. a sentence of 30 hours of community service for a minor theft charge
   c. an award of one million dollars in punitive damages for a wrongful death act
   d. shock treatment to help condition a person not to be aroused sexually by the sight of young children.

30. One of the greatest weaknesses with retribution theory is _____.

   a. many offenders do not make rational choices
   b. many offenders have addictions
   c. it is difficult to determine what is just deserts (how much punishment is just)
   d. it is forward looking

TRUE/FALSE

1. Prior decisions that are relevant to deciding the current case are called precedents.
   a. true
   b. false

2. The doctrine of *stare decisis* generally requires judges to follow precedents established by equal or higher courts.
   a. true
   b. false

3. One way for a court to avoid a precedent is to distinguish the prior case.
   a. true
   b. false

4. The second set of numbers in a case/opinion citation is the date of the decision.
   a. true
   b. false

5. The first set of numbers in a case citation is the page number on which the case begins.
   a. true
   b. false

6. Most criminal laws in the U.S. are state laws.
   a. true
   b. false

7. Rehabilitation and prevention are prospective (looking to prevent future crime).
   a. true
   b. false

8. Principles of accomplice liability are part of the special part of the criminal law.
   a. true
   b. false

9. Crimes which are *malum in se* are more harmful and blameworthy than crimes which are *malum prohibitum*
   a. true
   b. false

10. The federal government and most states utilize common-law crimes exclusively.
    a. true
    b. false

11. *Stare decisis* is an absolute rule with no exceptions.
    a. true
    b. false

12. Ordinances may conflict with state law.
    a. true
    b. false

13. The constitution limits the ability of agencies to create criminal laws and punishments.
    a. true
    b. false

14. The American criminal law is based on the common law of Spain.
    a. true
    b. false

15. Punishing an individual to make an example of him and deter others from committing more crimes is called specific deterrence.
    a. true
    b. false

16. The elements of the crimes of rape or murder would be found in the special part of the criminal law.
    a. true
    b. false

17. Misdemeanors are crimes punishable by more than one year incarceration in a local jail.
    a. true
    b. false

Study Guide

18. Driving on the left side of the road is an example of an offense that is *malum prohibitum*.
    a. true
    b. false

19. Code jurisdictions are those that have kept common-law offenses.
    a. true
    b. false

20. Legislators are free to engage in retroactive criminal lawmaking as it is within the specific authority of the legislative branch to be lawmakers.
    a. true
    b. false

21. The Model Penal Code has been followed by all fifty states, but not by the federal government.
    a. true
    b. false

22. The rule of law means that government is limited in its ability to pass laws by considerations of fairness and liberty.
    a. true
    b. false

23. Since the 1980s, rehabilitation and treatment have been emphasized as the primary criminal punishment.
    a. true
    b. false

24. A regulation is the government placing a burden on a behavior to discourage it, without necessarily punishing the behavior.
    a. true
    b. false

25. A license is a user fee intended to discourage behavior.
    a. true
    b. false

FILL-IN-THE-BLANK

1. Sets of three dots in writing indicating that some material from quoted material has been omitted are called _____.

2. The party who appeals an adverse judgment or decision is called the _____.

3. A _____ is a private wrong for which a party can be sued.

4. The general principle that the government is bound to follow the law is called _____.

5. The rule of statutory construction which requires judges to narrowly construe the statute to the letter of the law is called _____.

6. _____ are violations of state and federal agency rules.

7. A _____ is a private party who brings a suit.

8. Monetary awards against a private party to punish them for wrongdoing are _____.

9. When an appellate court agrees with the decision of the court immediately below it, we say it has _____ the lower court decision.

10. When a case is _____, it is sent back down to a lower court for further proceedings, in accordance with the appellate court's decision.

11. The _____ part of the criminal law specifies principles that apply to all crimes.

12. Larceny, arson, burglary, and theft are classified as crimes against _____.

13. Judge-made law, originally based on the common customs or traditions of the people, is called the _____ law.

14. Today, most new crimes are created by the legislature by passing _____.

15. _____ is when someone is blameworthy and society decides to express its condemnation through a criminal conviction.

ESSAY

1. Describe the main sources of criminal law. Give examples of each.

2. Describe, define, compare, and contrast common law and code jurisdictions. Trace the evolution from a predominantly common-law nation to a predominantly code nation.

3. Describe and compare the power of judges, legislators, and administrative agencies to make criminal law. Discuss what limitations and constraints each have in making laws.

4. Describe the goals of punishment and trace the trends in punishment.

5. Discuss the assumptions which underlie retribution and deterrence theory. What theory do you feel best justifies criminal punishment?

CHAPTER 1 ANSWER KEY

Multiple Choice

1. a	2. c	3. b	4. d	5. a
6. c	7. a	8. a	9. b	10. c
11. a	12. b	13. c	14. b	15. b
16. a	17. b	18. c	19. a	20. d
21. a	22. b	23. b	24. a	25. c
26. d	27. c	28. c	29. b	30. c

True/False

1. T	2. T	3. T	4. F	5. F
6. T	7. T	8. F	9. T	10. F
11. F	12. F	13. T	14. F	15. F
16. T	17. F	18. T	19. F	20. F
21. F	22. T	23. F	24. T	25. F

Fill-in-the-Blank

1. ellipsis	2. appellant	3. tort
4. principle of legality	5. rule of lenity	6. Administrative crimes
7. plaintiff	8. punitive damages	9. affirmed
10. remanded	11. general	12. property
13. common	14. statutes or codes	15. Culpable

CHAPTER 2
CONSTITUTIONAL LIMITATIONS ON CRIMINAL LAW

LEARNING OBJECTIVES

After studying this chapter, students will understand that:

- In a constitutional democracy, there are limits placed on the power of the government to create crimes.

- Retroactive statutes, called *ex post facto* laws, are unconstitutional. These laws criminalize innocent acts, increase punishments for a crime, and take away a defense that was available to a defendant when the crime was committed.

- The ban on *ex post facto* laws protects private individuals by giving them a fair warning about what criminal behavior is and banning legislators from passing arbitrary and vindictive legislation.

- According to the U.S. Supreme Court, vague laws deny individuals their right to "due process" in both federal and state criminal justice.

- The variety of human behavior and the limits of human imagination make it impossible for lawmakers to predict all the variations that might arise under the provisions of statutes.

- Equal protection under the law doesn't require the government to treat everybody exactly alike.

- Criminals can be classified based on their prior criminal record, but the classification of criminals based on race falls under strict scrutiny and is never justified.

- The First Amendment rights to freedom of speech, religion, and associations can't be banned as crimes.

- Obscenity, profanity, libel, slander, fighting words, and expressions that pose a clear and present danger aren't protected by the First Amendment.

- The constitutional right to privacy bans "all governmental invasions of the sanctity of a man's home and the privacies of life."

- The cruel and unusual punishments clause bans "barbaric" punishments and punishments that are disproportionate to the crime.

- It's cruel and unusual punishment to execute the mentally retarded and criminals who committed their crimes as juveniles.

KEY TERMS AND CONCEPTS

- ***ex post facto* laws**—laws passed after the occurrence of the conduct constituting the crime; p. 48

- **void-for-vagueness doctrine**—the principle that a statute violates due process if it doesn't clearly define crime and punishment in advance; p. 50

- **void-for-overbreadth doctrine**—the principle that a statute is unconstitutional if its definition of undesirable behavior includes conduct protected under the U.S. Constitution; p. 56

- **chilling effect**—when people hesitate to express themselves because they fear criminal prosecution even though the Constitution protects their speech; p. 56

- **right to privacy**—a right that bans "all governmental invasions of the sanctity of a man's home and the privacies of life;" p. 60

- **barbaric punishments**—punishment no longer considered acceptable; p. 64

- **principle of proportionality**—a principle of law stating that the punishment must be proportional to the crime committed; p. 65

CHAPTER OUTLINE

I. Constitutional limits on criminal law
    A. The Constitution limits what the government can make criminal and directs how legislation should be enacted to protect individual's rights.
    B. Chapter covers the following limitations:
        1. *Ex post facto* laws
        2. Due process of laws
        3. Equal protection of laws
        4. Free speech, association, press, and religion
        5. Privacy
        6. Cruel and unusual punishment

II. *Ex Post Facto* Laws
    A. The principle "no crime without law; no punishment without law" (meaning no retroactive lawmaking) is so fundamental that it is embodied within the U.S. Constitution. Article 1 Section 9 prohibits legislatures from passing *ex post facto* laws.

B. **Kinds of *Ex Post Facto* Laws**
   1. Statues that criminalize innocent acts after they are committed
   2. Statutes which increase the punishment for a crime after it was committed—*Garner v. Jones* (2000)
   3. Statutes which take away a defense that was available to the defendant when the crime was committed
C. **The Purpose of the Ban on *Ex Post Facto* Laws**
   1. Give fair warnings to private individuals
   2. Prevent arbitrary government action

III. **Due Process**
   A. **Void-for-Vagueness:** Laws which are too vague violate a person's rights to due process. Because vague laws fail to warn a person of what the law is, or allow officials to arbitrarily decide what the law means, they deprive individuals of their right to life, liberty, or property.
   B. **The Aims of the Void-for-Vagueness Doctrine**
      1. Failure to give fair warning to individuals as to what the law prohibits
      2. Allow arbitrary and discriminatory application of the law—*Lanzetta v. New Jersey*
   C. **Defining Vagueness**
      1. What is fair notice?
         a. "Would an ordinary, reasonable person know that what he was doing was criminal?"
      2. Minimal guidelines to govern law enforcement
         a. Controlling law enforcement has recently been given more priority in the vagueness analysis than whether fair notice is provided.
      3. Presumption of constitutionality requires challengers to prove the law is vague rather than the government having to prove that it is not too vague.
   D. *Case: State v. Metzger*

IV. **Equal Protection of the Laws**
   A. The 14th Amendment prohibits states from denying a person equal protection of law. States don't have to treat everybody the same. Statutes can in fact treat classes of persons differently, but whether the statute will pass constitutional muster depends on what the classification is, how narrowly the statute is crafted, and how badly and why the state needs to treat the people in the class differently.
   B. Race-based classifications—Courts must look at statute with strict scrutiny. Thus, such classifications always violate the constitution.
   C. Gender-based classifications—Courts must look at statute with heightened scrutiny. State must show a "fair and substantial relationship between the classification and a legitimate state end."
   D. Other classifications—Courts must show that there is a rational basis between the classification and the state's need to treat those falling in that classification differently.

V. **The Bill of Rights and Criminal Law**—The Bill of Rights bans defining certain kinds of behavior as criminal.

VI. **Free Speech**—First Amendment to U.S. Constitution
   A. Application
      1. Speech is broad in scope, including expressive conduct and giving money to candidates.
      2. Applies to federal government and to states
      3. Free speech is a fundamental right with preferred status. (States need compelling interest to limit it.)
      4. Some types of speech are not protected, and the government can make time, place, and manner restrictions on them.
   B. Void-for-Overbreadth Doctrine—When a statute prohibits something that the constitution protects, the statute is said to be overbroad. The concern is that people will refrain from doing or saying things they have a lawful right to do and say because they are afraid they will be prosecuted. The concern then becomes that the overbroad statute will have a chilling effect on people's behavior.
      1. *R.A.V. v. City of St. Paul*
   C. *Case: People v. Rokicki*
   D. *Case: Barns v. Glen Theater, Inc et. al.*
   E. *Case: Texas v. Johnson*

VII. **The Right to Privacy**
   A. Application
      1. Right to privacy is found within the "penumbra" of the Constitution, not in any specific clause or Amendment. State constitutions may have specific provisions regarding the right to privacy.
      2. Right to privacy bans "government invasions into sanctity of home and privacies of life."
      3. Fundamental right—Each state has to show compelling state interest in order to justify invading this right.
   B. *Case: Griswold v. Connecticut*
   C. *Case: Stanley v. Georgia*
   D. *Case: Lawrence v. Texas*

VIII. **Cruel and Unusual Punishment**
   A. **Barbaric Punishments**—Punishments which are no longer acceptable in a civilized society; thus, as society evolves, what has been considered barbaric, has likewise changed.
      1. Death itself isn't cruel and unusual, but if it involves unnecessary mutilation of the body or pain, it is cruel.
   B. **Proportional Punishments**
      1. Principle of Proportionality—The punishment should fit the crime. Very harsh punishments, which are completely out of line with the severity of the crime, violate the principle of proportionality.
      2. Federal (*Weems*) and state (*Robinson*) ban on disproportional punishment.

C. **The Death Penalty: "Death is Different"**
   1. Although there are non-capital crimes which allow the death penalty, currently, no one ever gets the death penalty for those crimes.
   2. *Coker v. Georgia*—The court prohibited the death penalty for rape of adult woman.
   3. *Case: State v. Wilson*
D. **The Death Penalty for the Mentally Retarded**—*Atkins v. Virginia* (2002). The court noted a consistent and pervasive change in public opinion against executing retarded offenders and held that it was now cruel and unusual punishment to execute retarded offenders. Also, retarded offenders aren't as blameworthy (culpable) or subject to deterrence as others.
E. **The Death Penalty for Juveniles**—*Roper v. Simmons* (2004). The court overruled earlier opinions and decided that due to "evolving standards of decency in a civilized society," it was now cruel and unusual punishment to execute offenders who committed their crimes before turning 18 years old.
F. **Imprisonment**
   1. Lack of consensus on whether prison sentences have to be proportionate to the crime committed
   2. Application would be for mandatory minimum and three strikes type of sentences.
   3. *Case: Ewing v. California*

CHAPTER SUMMARY

Because the United States is a constitutional democracy, there are limits to the power of state and federal governments to create crimes. These limitations are found within the U.S. Constitution and the individual state constitutions.

The purposes of banning *ex post facto* and vague criminal statutes are to give fair warning to individuals as to what the law prohibits and to prevent arbitrary enforcement by public officials. The constitutional basis for banning laws so vague that reasonable private individuals and public officials can't understand them is that such laws deprive individuals of life, liberty, or property without due process of law.

The U.S. Constitution doesn't guarantee that criminal laws treat everybody exactly alike; it does command that classifying people or behavior differently be reasonable (or have a rational basis). Classifications based on gender are subject to a heightened scrutiny by the court and the state must show a substantial relationship to the legitimate state interest. Classifications based upon race or ethnicity are subject to strict scrutiny (the highest level of scrutiny) and are generally always unconstitutional.

Under the First Amendment to the U.S. Constitution, the guarantee of free speech is a fundamental right. Government action infringing on rights that are deemed fundamental must be shown to be more than reasonable. The action must be justified by showing that it furthers a compelling governmental interest. According to the U.S. Supreme Court, some kinds of nonverbal, expressive conduct are speech; some words aren't "speech," and some speech isn't protected by the guarantee of free speech. Obscenity and fighting words are examples of speech not protected by the First Amendment.

The word privacy doesn't appear in the U.S. Constitution, but the U.S. Supreme Court has indicated in one case that it lies within the "penumbra" of the Constitution—meaning that it is implicit in several clauses of the Bill of Rights (the first ten Amendments to the U.S. Constitution). The Court has dealt with privacy issues in matters concerning family life, reproduction, and child rearing. Recently the court examined whether statutes criminalizing consensual homosexual conduct between adults violated the right to privacy. In deciding that it did, the court in *Lawrence v. Texas* (2003) overruled an earlier 1986 decision.

The U.S. Supreme Court has interpreted the ban on cruel and unusual punishments to include barbaric punishments and punishments disproportionate to crimes. The death penalty is valid if certain constitutional rules are followed. Recently the Court has looked to the changing standards and sentiments of a civilized community in determining that executing retarded individuals and individuals who committed their crimes before they turned 18 years old both violate the ban on cruel and unusual punishment.

PRACTICE TEST BANK

MULTIPLE CHOICE

1. The U.S. is a _____.

    a. constitutional monarchy
    b. pure democracy
    c. parliamentary style government
    d. constitutional democracy

2. Damages to reputation in the form of spoken words are known as _____.

    a. libel
    b. slander
    c. profanity
    d. obscenity

3. Which of the following would violate the ban on *ex post facto* laws?

    a. retroactive criminal statute
    b. vague statute giving too much power to government
    c. statute broadly regulating protective speech
    d. providing death penalty for petty theft

4. The primary considerations in analysis of laws under the void-for-vagueness doctrine are _____.

    a. retroactivity and potential for punishing innocent people
    b. legislative encroachment on the judiciary and legislative tyranny
    c. infringement of First and Seventh Amendment rights
    d. reasonably fair notice and potential for arbitrary or discriminatory enforcement

5. In a constitutional democracy, _____.

    a. the will of the majority is the supreme law
    b. the power of the majority and government are limited by the Constitution
    c. the legislature has the final say on the meaning of the Constitution
    d. the Constitution can be amended just like any statute

6. The _____ Amendment requires that states provide equal protection of laws.

   a. First
   b. Sixth
   c. Eighth
   d. Fourteenth

7. The _____ Amendment requires the states provide due process of laws.

   a. First
   b. Eighth
   c. Fourteenth
   d. Fifteenth

8. Except when dealing with fundamental rights and classifications based on race, ethnicity, gender, etc., the government can meet an equal protection challenge to a law by _____.

   a. passing the strict scrutiny test
   b. meeting the requirement of heightened scrutiny
   c. showing that the law has a rational basis
   d. showing that the law furthers a compelling government interest

9. The First Amendment offers protection from government for _____.

   a. some expressive conduct as well as some spoken or written words
   b. every form of spoken or written word
   c. every form of expressive conduct
   d. some spoken or written words but no expressive conduct

10. The First Amendment protects which of the following?

    a. obscenity
    b. profanity
    c. expressive conduct
    d. slander

11. Statutes that ban some forms of unprotected speech, but which _____ the exercise of some protected speech, may be unconstitutional under the void-for-overbreadth doctrine.

    a. chill or deter
    b. can lead to arbitrary enforcement against
    c. promote or facilitate
    d. condone or ratify

12. In *People v. Rokicki* (1999), the defendant argued he was being unconstitutionally punished for his beliefs. The Illinois Supreme Court stated that the defendant's First Amendment challenge to the hate crime law was _____.

    a. invalid because he allowed his beliefs to motivate unreasonable conduct
    b. upheld because he was being punished because of his beliefs
    c. invalid because his beliefs were totally irrelevant to the case
    d. upheld because his conduct did not go beyond mere expression

13. In *Texas v. Johnson* (1989), the Court held that burning an American flag as part of a political protest could _____.

    a. be punished because it involved conduct
    b. be punished because the American flag is a unique symbol
    c. not be punished because it was protected expressive conduct
    d. not be punished because it was pure speech

14. Even though the word "_____" does not appear anywhere in the U.S. Constitution, the U.S. Supreme Court has held that there is such a fundamental right.

    a. liberty
    b. privacy
    c. property
    d. attainder

15. In *Lawrence v. Texas* (2003), the U.S. Supreme Court _____ its prior decision in *Bowers v. Hardwick* (1986).

    a. affirmed
    b. reversed
    c. overruled
    d. remanded

16. The ban on cruel and unusual punishment is found in the _____ Amendment.

    a. Fifth
    b. Sixth
    c. Seventh
    d. Eighth

17. In *State v. Wilson* (1996), the Louisiana Supreme Court distinguished the U.S. Supreme Court decision in *Coker v. Georgia* (1997) because the Wilson case involved _____.

    a. the death of a child
    b. the rape of a child
    c. a child killing another child
    d. a child raping another child

18. In *Stanley v. Georgia* (1969), the Court held that _____.

    a. a prosecution for mere possession of pornography in one's own home violates a fundamental right to be free from unwanted governmental intrusion into one's privacy
    b. a prosecution for homosexual conduct violates a fundamental right to be free from unwanted governmental intrusion into one's privacy
    c. a prosecution for pornography is constitutional in that obscenity is not within the area of constitutionally protected speech or press
    d. a prosecution for pornography violates equal protection of laws

19. The case of *Griswold v. Connecticut* (1965) involved _____.

    a. the use of contraceptives by a married couple
    b. the inter-racial marriage of a couple
    c. the right to free speech
    d. the right to be free from cruel and unusual punishment

20. The case of *Roper v. Simmons* (2004) involved _____.

    a. the application of the death penalty for a mentally retarded offender
    b. the application of the death penalty for a crime of rape
    c. the application of the death penalty for a juvenile offender
    d. the application of the electric chair as a method of execution under the death penalty

21. Barbaric punishment are those punishments which _____.

    a. violate international law
    b. are considered no longer acceptable to a civilized society
    c. involve imposing death to the offender
    d. are less severe than cruel and unusual punishment

22. Which of the following would be deemed to violate the principle of proportionality?

    a. imposing the death penalty for a particularly heinous murder
    b. imposing the death penalty for spitting on the sidewalk
    c. impose a fine for a violation
    d. impose a fine for a status offense

23. In *Ewing v. California* (2003), the court held that _____.

    a. the Eighth Amendment's principle of proportionality prohibits a sentence of 25 years to life for grand theft
    b. the Eighth Amendment's protection against barbaric punishment prohibits a sentence of 25 years to life for grand theft
    c. Ewing's sentence of 25 years to life for grand theft is not grossly disproportionate and doesn't violate the Eighth Amendment
    d. the Eighth Amendment does not contain a proportionality clause

24. The void-for-overbreadth doctrine prohibits _____.

    a. vague laws
    b. laws which prohibit constitutionally protected speech
    c. laws which retroactively make behavior a crime
    d. laws which have no limits on the arbitrariness and discretion of police officers

25. In *R.A.V. v. City of St. Paul*, the U.S. Supreme Court invalidated a Minnesota hate crime ordinance because _____.

    a. it allowed the proponents of racial tolerance and equality to use fighting words but not the opponents of racial tolerance
    b. it dealt only with conduct and not speech
    c. it dealt only with speech and not conduct
    d. it was constitutionally vague and allowed police unlimited discretion in interpreting the statute

26. The rule of law and principle of legality require that people be punished only _____.

    a. for violating properly enacted laws
    b. if they had some culpable *mens rea*
    c. if they personally did the criminal act
    d. if their acts harm society

27. Which of the following methods of execution is not cruel and unusual punishment?

    a. crucifixion
    b. beheading
    c. drawing and quartering
    d. lethal injection

28. Which of the following scenarios raises issues of disproportionate punishment?

    a. a statute imposing a 20 year sentence for a third shoplifting offense
    b. a statute allowing for a mandatory minimum sentence for robbery
    c. a statute making homelessness punishable by 30 days jail
    d. a statute requiring a shoplifter wear a placard stating, "I am a thief."

29. The _____ Amendment provides for the right to associate and assemble with those of your choosing.

    a. First
    b. Fourth
    c. Fifth
    d. Fourteenth

30. The _____ case dealt with the state's ability to limit nude dancing.

    a. *Weems v. United States*
    b. *Gitlow v. New York*
    c. *Barnes v. Glen Theatre, Inc. et. al.*
    d. *People v. Rockiki*

TRUE/FALSE

1. Laws governing hate crimes, such as cross burnings, will always run afoul of the First Amendment's free speech clause because they involve expressive conduct.
    a. true
    b. false

2. The ban on *ex post facto* laws is designed to prevent excessively vague laws.
    a. true
    b. false

3. The void-for-vagueness doctrine totally prohibits any vagueness or uncertainty in laws.
    a. true
    b. false

4. Statues that criminalize innocent acts after they're committed violate the ban against *ex post facto* laws.
   a. true
   b. false

5. Laws involving gender classifications are tested under the rational basis test.
   a. true
   b. false

6. Yelling "fire" in a crowded movie theater is an example of non-protected speech known as clear and present danger.
   a. true
   b. false

7. The U.S. Supreme Court has held that states may not prohibit nude dancing.
   a. true
   b. false

8. Fighting words are not protected by the First Amendment.
   a. true
   b. false

9. The constitutional right to equal protection of laws means that the government cannot treat people differently.
   a. true
   b. false

10. According to the U.S. Supreme Court, beheading would not be considered cruel and unusual punishment.
    a. true
    b. false

11. According to the U.S. Supreme Court, imposing any jail sentence for a status offense, such as being a drug addict, would be cruel and unusual punishment.
    a. true
    b. false

12. The U.S. Supreme Court has disallowed the use of the death penalty for the rape of an adult victim.
    a. true
    b. false

13. In *Stanley v. Georgia*, the U.S. Supreme Court struck down a statute criminalizing personal adult possession of obscene material in the privacy of the home.
    a.   true
    b.   false

14. The Sixth Amendment prohibits cruel and unusual punishment.
    a.   true
    b.   false

15. Executing people who are mentally retarded has been held as a violation to the ban on cruel and unusual punishment.
    a.   true
    b.   false

16. In *Atkins v. Virginia,* the U.S. Supreme Court held that imposing the death penalty on people who committed murder while a juvenile violates the ban on cruel and unusual punishment.
    a.   true
    b.   false

17. In deciding whether executing juvenile offenders violated the ban on cruel and unusual punishment, the court looked to evolving standards of decency.
    a.   true
    b.   false

18. Lengthy imprisonment sentences have generally been found to violate the principle of proportionality.
    a.   true
    b.   false

19. Hate crimes violate the First Amendment.
    a.   true
    b.   false

20. Broadly written laws that have an impact on protected speech and press are invalid if they are deemed overbroad.
    a.   true
    b.   false

21. Freedom of speech and expression are fundamental rights.
    a.   true
    b.   false

Study Guide

22. Under equal protection, racial classifications are subject to strict scrutiny.
    a. true
    b. false

23. Under equal protection, classifications based on age are subject to strict scrutiny.
    a. true
    b. false

24. Classifications based on gender are subject to normal scrutiny and require that the government have a rational basis in enacting such legislation.
    a. true
    b. false

25. There is a general consensus that a length of imprisonment which is disproportionate to the type and manner of crime which was committed violates the ban on cruel and unusual punishment.
    a. true
    b. false

FILL-IN-THE-BLANK

1. The Eighth Amendment principle of _____ requires that punishment fit the crime.

2. _____ is offensive, sexually explicit material which is not protected by the First Amendment.

3. Making a statement through acts or symbols is called _____ conduct.

4. Government classifications on the basis of race are subject to _____ by the courts.

5. The Equal Protection Clause and the Due Process Clause are found in the _____ Amendment.

6. The American form of government is described as a _____ democracy.

7. The doctrine which dictates that laws provide notice to individuals as to what behavior constitutes a crime is the _____ doctrine.

8. The doctrine which states that laws can't prohibit constitutionally protected behavior is the _____ doctrine.

9. Laws which limit speech are subject to strict scrutiny because they may have a _____ effect on a person's desire to speak freely.

10. The void-for-vagueness doctrine addresses the evil of _____ and discriminatory practices in criminal justice administration.

11. The constitutional right to privacy is found within the _____ of the Constitution.

12. There are two types of cruel and unusual punishment under the Eighth Amendment: _____ punishment and _____ punishment.

13. When a right is said to be "fundamental" and subject to heightened or strict scrutiny, the government must have a _____ interest in limiting behavior affecting that right.

14. Words that are likely to provoke the average person to retaliation and cause a breach of the peace are known as _____ words.

15. Damages to reputation expressed in print, writing, pictures, or signs are known as _____, whereas damages to reputation expressed in spoken words are known as _____.

ESSAY

1. What are the differences between the doctrines of void-for-vagueness and void-for-overbreadth? What are the primary concerns with each of these doctrines, and how do these doctrines address the concerns?

2. How have evolving standards of decency affected what citizens and the courts have decided to be cruel and unusual punishment?

3. Why does the court adopt different standards of scrutiny for rights it deems fundamental? What are the levels of scrutiny, and what must the government show in order to survive such scrutiny when enacting legislation?

4. Discuss when the court is likely to uphold a hate crime statute and when it will not, based on the decisions in *R.A.V. v. City of St. Paul* and *People v. Rokicki.*.

5. Trace and discuss the constitutional right to privacy from *Griswold v. Connecticut* through *Lawrence v. Texas*.

CHAPTER 2 ANSWER KEY

Multiple Choice

1. d	2. b	3. a	4. d	5. b
6. d	7. c	8. c	9. a	10. c
11. a	12. a	13. c	14. b	15. b
16. d	17. b	18. a	19. a	20. c
21. b	22. b	23. c	24. b	25. a
26. a	27. d	28. c	29. a	30. c

True/False

1. F	2. F	3. F	4. T	5. F
6. T	7. F	8. T	9. F	10. F
11. T	12. T	13. T	14. F	15. T
16. F	17. T	18. F	19. F	20. T
21. T	22. T	23. F	24. F	25. F

Fill-in-the-Blank

1. proportionality
2. Obscenity
3. expressive
4. strict scrutiny
5. Fourteenth
6. constitutional
7. void-for-vagueness
8. void-for-overbreadth
9. chilling
10. arbitrary
11. penumbra
12. barbarian; disproportionate
13. compelling
14. fighting
15. libel; slander

CHAPTER 3
THE GENERAL PRINCIPLES OF CRIMINAL LIABILITY: *ACTUS REUS*

LEARNING OBJECTIVES

After studying this chapter, students will understand that:

- The criminal act (*actus reus*) is just one of the five elements that the prosecution has to prove beyond a reasonable doubt to convict individual defendants.

- Offenses that don't require *mens rea* almost always include an attendant circumstance element.

- Criminal acts are physical bodily movements; criminal conduct is the combination of *actus reus* triggered by *mens rea*.

- Criminal law demands that intention turns into action.

- Every crime has to include at least one voluntary act.

- Status (race, age, sex, sexual orientation, ethnicity) can never qualify as *actus reus*.

- Failures to act can be *actus reus* when there's a legal duty to act.

- Possession is *not* action; it's a passive condition that can qualify as a criminal act.

KEY TERMS AND CONCEPTS

- **elements of a crime**—the parts of a crime that the prosecution must prove beyond a reasonable doubt, such as *actus reus, mens rea,* concurrence, causation, and bad result; p. 80

- ***actus reus***—the criminal act or the physical element in criminal liability; p. 81

- ***mens rea***—the state of mind the prosecution has to prove beyond a reasonable doubt; criminal intent from an evil mind; the mental element in crime, including purpose, knowledge, recklessness, and negligence; p. 81

- **attendant circumstances**—a circumstance connected to an act, an intent, and/or a result required to make an act criminal; p. 81

- **concurrence**—the requirement that *actus reus* must join with *mens rea* to produce criminal conduct or that conduct must cause a harmful result; p. 81

- **conduct crimes**—crimes requiring a criminal act triggered by criminal intent; p. 81

- **result crimes**—serious crimes that include causing a criminal harm in addition to the conduct itself (for example, criminal homicide); p. 82

- **manifest criminality**—the requirement in law that intentions have to turn into criminal deeds to be punishable; p. 83

- **status (as *actus reus*)**—who we are, as opposed to what we do; a condition that's not an action can't substitute for action as an element in crime; p. 87

- **criminal omission**—two forms: 1) mere failure to act or 2) failure to intervene in order to prevent a serious harm; p. 90

- **failure to report (criminal omission)**—one type of omission *actus reus*; p. 90

- **failure to intervene (criminal omission)**—one type of omission *actus reus*; p. 90

- **legal duty (in criminal omission)**—liability only for duties imposed by contract, statute, or "special relationships;" p. 90

- **"Good Samaritan" doctrine**—the doctrine that imposes a legal duty to render or summon aid for imperiled strangers; p. 91

- **American bystander rule**—there's no legal duty to rescue or call for help to aid someone who's in danger, even if helping poses no risk whatsoever to the potential rescuer; p. 91

- **legal fiction (in *actus reus*)**—treating something as a fact that's not a fact, if there's a good reason for doing so; p. 96

- **actual possession**—physical possession; on the possessor's person; p. 97

- **constructive possession**—legal possession or custody of an item or substance; p. 97

- **knowing possession**—awareness of physical possession; p. 97

- **mere possession**—physical possession; p. 97

CHAPTER OUTLINE

I. The Elements of Criminal Liability
    A. There are a number of general principles of criminal liability.
    B. The government must prove every element of the crime beyond a reasonable doubt.
    C. The Constitution requires a criminal act to prove criminal liability.
        1. A criminal act is the basis of the principle of *actus reus*.
        2. This is an element the prosecution has to prove beyond a reasonable doubt.
    D. Two types of crimes lead to criminal liability.
        1. Conduct crimes require proving three elements of crimes.
            a. *Actus reus* (criminal act)
            b. *Mens rea* (criminal intent)
            c. Concurrence (criminal act triggered by criminal intent)
        2. Result Crimes require proving five elements of crimes.
            a. *Actus reus*
            b. *Mens rea*
            c. Concurrence
                (1) *Actus reus* and *mens rea* produce criminal conduct.
                (2) The criminal conduct results in harm.
            d. Causation (must prove the criminal conduct produced criminal harm as defined in the criminal statute)
            e. Resulting harm (the specific result defined in the criminal code)
    E. Each element of crime relates to a general principle of criminal liability.

II. *Actus Reus*: The First Principle of Liability
    A. Every crime involves a criminal act, referred to as the *actus reus*. *Actus reus* is the first principle of criminal liability.
    B. Two requirements to prove *actus reus*
        1. Bodily movements resulted in criminal act.
        2. Bodily movements were voluntary.
    C. **Voluntary Acts**: Reasoning for the voluntary act requirement
        1. Criminal law punishes people.
        2. Criminal law can't punish without blame.
        3. There is no blame without responsibility.
        4. There is no responsibility without a voluntary act (free will).
        5. *Case: Brown v. State*
        6. *Case: King v. Cogdon*
        7. *Case: People v. Decina*
        8. *Case: State v. Jerrett*
    D. **Status** as a criminal act
        1. Act is what we do; status is who we are.
        2. Status is created in two ways.
            a. Voluntary act (first use of alcohol or other drug)
            b. Inherent (race, ethnicity, sex, age)

3. *Actus Reus* and the U.S. Constitution
      a. Punishment for status violates U.S. Constitution, Amendment VIII (cruel and unusual punishment), by the same reasoning a voluntary act is required by the principle of *actus reus*.
      b. *Case: Robinson v. California*

III. Omissions—Failure to act as a criminal act
  A. Two types of criminal omissions
      1. Failure to report (accident, income tax)
      2. Failure to intervene (call for help or rescue)
  B. It's wrong (but not always a crime) to stand by while bad things happen.
      1. Moral and legal duties differ.
      2. Failure to act is a criminal act only when there's a legal duty to act, created by:
         a. Statute
         b. Contract
         c. Special relationship
      3. Criminal liability exists only when both of the following are true:
         a. There's a legal duty to act.
         b. The legal duty is performed unreasonably.
      4. Failure to perform moral duties does not qualify as a criminal omission.
      5. Two approaches to creating and carrying out legal duties toward strangers in trouble
         a. Good Samaritan doctrine—legal duty to help or summon help for strangers in danger
         b. American bystander rule (most states)—no legal duty to rescue or summon help for strangers
      6. *Case: Commonwealth v. Pestinakas*
      7. *Case: People v. Oliver*
      8. *Case: State v. Miranda*
      9. *Story: Kitty Genovese Story*

IV. Possession
  A. Possession is a passive state, not a positive act.
  B. Legal fiction makes it an act for good policy reasons.
      1. Reduce crime
      2. Many times possession is the result of a voluntary act.
  C. Two aspects of possession
      1. Control of items and substances
         a. Actual (substance or item on the person)
         b. Constructive (control the stuff but not on the person)
      2. Awareness of control
         a. Knowing possession (the person knows they possess the stuff.)
         b. Mere possession (the stuff is physically on the person, but they don't know it.)

D. Kinds of possession
  1. Control: actual and constructive
  2. Awareness: knowing and mere
E. *Case: Miller v. State*
F. *Case: Porter v. State*
G. *Case: State v. Kimberley*

CHAPTER SUMMARY

The prosecution is required to prove every element of the crime beyond a reasonable doubt. One basic principle of criminal liability is the requirement of a criminal act, which the prosecution has to prove beyond a reasonable doubt.

Two types of crime based on their elements are crimes of criminal conduct and crimes of criminal conduct causing criminal harms. Crimes of criminal conduct have a mental state and an act triggered by the mental state. The concurrence element requires that the act be caused or triggered by the intent (*mens rea*). Intending to commit a crime is not a crime because it hasn't ripened into a criminal act (*actus reus*). Crimes of criminal conduct causing harm have the additional elements of causation and harm. The act must cause the harm.

The *actus reus* can be a positive act (commission) or omission to act. A criminal act has to be a voluntary bodily movement because we can't blame people for their involuntary acts. Actions refer to what we *do*; status or condition refers to who or what we *are*. Some conditions we're born with; and others we produce by our acts. Making a disease a crime violates the cruel and unusual punishment clause of the Eighth Amendment to the U.S. Constitution. It's a criminal act to stand by and do nothing when there's a legal duty to act. A legal duty to act can be imposed by civil or criminal statutes, the common law, a contract, or a special relationship. *Actus reus* does not include a failure to do what one may have a "moral duty" to do.

There are two types of criminal omissions: failure to report and failure to intervene. Criminal omissions create criminal liability only when a legal duty is not reasonably performed.

Possession is a passive state, but it can qualify as a criminal act when properly defined by law. There are a number of aspects or possible elements of possession crimes: 1) physical control of an item; 2) awareness of physical control of some item; and 3) awareness of the nature of the item (whether it is contraband or not). Actual possession means the item is on your person or within your reach. Constructive possession means the item is under your control but not on your person or within your reach. Things you leave at your home, by putting them in your safe (for which you have the combination), are constructively possessed. Mere possession means you have possession of it, and know you have possession, but don't know the nature of the item (that it is contraband). Knowing possession means that you knowingly possess the item and know that the item is contraband. Most states require proof that the possessor knew the item was contraband before a conviction can be obtained.

PRACTICE TEST BANK

MULTIPLE CHOICE

1. To obtain a conviction, the prosecution must prove every element of the offense beyond _____.

    a. probable cause
    b. a reasonable suspicion
    c. clear and convincing evidence
    d. a reasonable doubt

2. Based on the elements of crime, there are two types of crime _____.

    a. crimes of criminal conduct and harm
    b. crimes of criminal intent and *mens rea*
    c. crimes of criminal conduct and *actus reus*
    d. overt and covert

3. The essence of the principle of *actus reus* is _____.

    a. intention
    b. act
    c. concurrence
    d. contingency

4. The principle of *mens rea* involves _____.

    a. intent
    b. act
    c. concurrence
    d. harm

5. The requirement of manifest criminality before there is punishment means that _____.

    a. intent alone, without an act, is not a crime
    b. an act alone, without intent, is not a crime
    c. harm alone, without causation, is not a crime
    d. causation alone, without harm, is not a crime

6. To be criminal, an act must be _____.

   a. objective
   b. peremptory
   c. voluntary
   d. the cause of the harm

7. In *Powell v. Texas* (1968), the Court held that under the Eighth Amendment, an alcoholic _____.

   a. could not be guilty of any crime committed while intoxicated
   b. was not entitled to a constitutional defense of chronic alcoholism
   c. could not be guilty of public intoxication
   d. was not capable of a voluntary act while intoxicated

8. In *Robinson v. California* (1962), the Court specifically held that under the Eighth Amendment, government could not make it a crime to be _____.

   a. addicted to the use of narcotics
   b. a hypochondriac
   c. a compulsive gambler
   d. a nymphomaniac

9. Under the Eighth Amendment, government cannot punish someone for a/n _____.

   a. status, disease, or condition
   b. crime that has no *mens rea* element
   c. act that is not involuntary
   d. crime that is the result of a psychological compulsion

10. Acts committed during somnambulism or automatism cannot be criminal because the acts _____.
    a. are not reflexive
    b. do not indicate the personality of the offender
    c. are not voluntary
    d. are not spontaneous

11. The term *actus reus* means evil _____.

    a. act
    b. mind
    c. intent
    d. result

12. The element of concurrence means that the _____.

    a. act must cause the intent
    b. harm must flow from intent
    c. intent must cause the act
    d. harm must flow from the act

13. As compared to crimes of criminal conduct, crimes of criminal harm have two additional elements, _____.

    a. concurrence and victimization
    b. causation and harm
    c. conspicuity and damage
    d. contiguity and result

14. The three elements of crimes of criminal conduct are *actus reus*, *mens rea*, and _____.

    a. conduct
    b. concurrence
    c. consistence
    d. contagion

15. In terms of *actus reus*, an omission is a _____.

    a. duty
    b. mistake
    c. failure to act
    d. failure to think

16. A legal duty to act is an example of a criminal element called _____.

    a. (attendant) circumstances
    b. *mens rea*
    c. *actus reus*
    d. harm

17. Under the Good Samaritan doctrine, a person has a legal duty to _____.

    a. report all crimes to the police
    b. investigate crimes they witness
    c. render or summon aid for people in danger
    d. help the poor avoid economic crimes

18. A legal fiction is a legal rule that _____.

    a. assumes the existence of fact that does not exist
    b. distributes the burden of proof
    c. defines the role of the jury in fact-finding
    d. can be overcome by evidence

19. Legally, possession is deemed to be a type of _____.

    a. *mens rea*
    b. harm
    c. act
    d. concurrence

20. A person who is carrying an item in their pocket, purse, or backpack is in _____ possession of the container and items therein.

    a. constructive
    b. fictional
    c. derivative
    d. actual

21. To be guilty of possession of contraband, most states require that the prosecution prove that the defendant knew _____.

    a. the quantity of the item possessed
    b. the nature of the item possessed
    c. that the item was going to be sold for profit
    d. that the person who gave it to him/her had no right to possess it

22. In contrast to the Good Samaritan doctrine, the American bystander rule imposes _____.

    a. less duty to help complete strangers
    b. no duty to help one's own children
    c. more duty to assist others
    d. duties only when felonies are involved

23. The two main types of criminal omissions are failure to _____.

    a. report and intervene
    b. act and think
    c. prevent and conclude
    d. act subjectively and objectively

24. A person leaves their heroin at home locked in a safe to which he or she has the combination. The person then goes to the train station. At the train station, this is an example of _____ possession.

    a. fractional
    b. joint
    c. constructive
    d. actual

25. If a person does not know the nature of the item they possess, this is called _____ possession.

    a. fictional
    b. constructive
    c. mere
    d. actual

26. An omission to act is a crime, only if there is a _____ duty to act.

    a. fictional
    b. moral
    c. actual
    d. legal

27. The requirement that there be an act element prevents government from punishing people _____.

    a. for bad thoughts only
    b. for their conduct
    c. for the harm they cause
    d. who lack concurrence

28. The requirement that people be punished for acts rather than diseases, conditions, or status grows out of the _____ Amendment.

    a. Fourth
    b. Sixth
    c. Eighth
    d. Ninth

Study Guide

29. The people who watched from their apartments while Kitty Genovese was being murdered in the street and failed to aid her or call the police were not guilty of any crime because they _____.

   a. could not be sure the police would arrive in time
   b. knew the attacker was armed
   c. did not know the identity of the attacker
   d. had no legal duty to aid her or call the police

30. A legal duty can arise from statutes, contracts, and _____.

   a. special relationships
   b. manumissions
   c. forfeitures
   d. discretion

TRUE/FALSE

1. The *actus reus* is the mental element of a crime.
   a. true
   b. false

2. The concurrence element means that the mental element must cause the harm.
   a. true
   b. false

3. The prosecution must prove every element of the crime beyond a reasonable doubt to get a conviction.
   a. true
   b. false

4. The *mens rea* is the harm element of a crime.
   a. true
   b. false

5. To be guilty of a criminal harm offense, the defendant must have caused the harm.
   a. true
   b. false

6. Crimes of criminal conduct have no concurrence element.
   a. true
   b. false

Chapter 3: The General Principles of Criminal Liability—*Actus Reus*

7. The term *actus reus* means evil act.
    a. true
    b. false

8. Under the Model Penal Code, to be guilty of an omission to act, the act must be one that the defendant was physically capable of performing.
    a. true
    b. false

9. Somnambulism is sleepwalking.
    a. true
    b. false

10. A reflex or spasm is a voluntary act.
    a. true
    b. false

11. In *Robinson v. California,* the U.S. Supreme Court held that governments may omit the *actus reus* element when defining crimes.
    a. true
    b. false

12. In *Powell v. Texas*, the Court held that the government cannot punish an alcoholic for any crimes committed while intoxicated.
    a. true
    b. false

13. Government cannot punish a person solely for their status, condition, or disease.
    a. true
    b. false

14. A failure to act is termed an omission.
    a. true
    b. false

15. A failure to act can be a crime only if there is a legal duty to do the act.
    a. true
    b. false

16. All moral duties are also legal duties.
    a. true
    b. false

17. The Good Samaritan doctrine imposes more duties to assist than does the American bystander rule.
    a. true
    b. false

18. A contract cannot create a legal duty to act.
    a. true
    b. false

19. Most states punish mere possession of contraband.
    a. true
    b. false

20. If an item is in a defendant's pocket, he is in actual possession of that item.
    a. true
    b. false

21. The concept of manifest criminality requires that the defendant's acts cause harm.
    a. true
    b. false

22. A legal fiction is something that is always true.
    a. true
    b. false

23. The mere presence of the accused on shared premises where contraband is found is, by itself, not enough to prove ownership or possession.
    a. true
    b. false

24. Knowing possession means that the person knows such possession is illegal.
    a. true
    b. false

25. The ban on cruel and unusual punishment is found in the Eighth Amendment.
    a. true
    b. false

FILL-IN-THE-BLANK

1. Another term for sleepwalking is _____.

2. The _____ is the act element of the crime.

3. The _____ is the mental element of the crime.

4. The _____ element requires that the mental element cause the act.

5. If a person commits an act during a state of automatism, the act is probably not a crime because the act is not _____.

6. The prosecution must prove every _____ of the crime beyond a reasonable doubt.

7. A failure to act is called a/n _____.

8. A failure to act is not a crime unless there is a/n _____ duty to do the act.

9. Persons have a broad duty to assist others under the _____ rule.

10. Under the _____ rule, people have little or no duty to assist strangers in peril.

11. In _____, the Court held that a person could not be punished for being a drug addict.

12. Possessing an item but not knowing the nature of that item is called _____ possession.

13. Although it may be a legal fiction, possession is deemed to be a form of _____.

14. Before it can be a crime, most states require that possession be _____ rather than just mere possession.

15. If a person leaves an item at home and goes elsewhere, they can still be in _____ possession of that item.

ESSAY

1. Explain why only voluntary acts are crimes. Be sure to provide examples.

2. Compare and contrast actual and constructive possession. Provide examples of each.

3. Compare and contrast knowing and mere possession. Provide examples of each.

4. Under what circumstances can an omission to act be deemed the *actus reus* of a crime? Be sure to provide examples.

5. Compare and contrast the Good Samaritan doctrine and the American bystander rule.

Chapter 3: The General Principles of Criminal Liability—*Actus Reus*

CHAPTER 3 ANSWER KEY

Multiple Choice

1. d	2. a	3. b	4. a	5. a
6. c	7. b	8. a	9. a	10. c
11. a	12. c	13. b	14. b	15. c
16. a	17. c	18. a	19. c	20. d
21. b	22. a	23. a	24. c	25. c
26. d	27. a	28. c	29. d	30. a

True/False

1. F	2. F	3. T	4. F	5. T
6. F	7. T	8. T	9. T	10. F
11. F	12. F	13. T	14. T	15. T
16. F	17. T	18. F	19. F	20. T
21. F	22. F	23. T	24. F	25. T

Fill-in-the-Blank

1. somnambulism
2. *actus reus*
3. *mens rea*
4. concurrence
5. voluntary
6. element
7. omission
8. legal
9. Good Samaritan
10. American bystander
11. *Robinson v. California*
12. mere
13. *actus reus*
14. knowing
15. constructive

CHAPTER 4
THE GENERAL PRINCIPLES OF CRIMINAL LIABILITY: *MENS REA*, CONCURRENCE, AND CAUSATION

LEARNING OBJECTIVES

After studying this chapter, students will understand that:

- Most crimes include a mental element.

- It's right and reasonable to punish only those who we can blame for committing crimes.

- The principle of *mens rea* is ancient and highly complex.

- Proving "state of mind" is difficult.

- Subjective and objective fault satisfy the mental element in criminal liability.

- General intent is the minimum requirement for all criminal conduct.

- Specific intent applies to result crimes.

- The Model Penal Code identifies four mental states—purposely, knowingly, recklessly, and negligently.

- Strict liability imposes criminal liability without subjective or objective fault.

- All crimes, except for strict liability offenses, are subject to the principle of concurrence.

- Causation only applies to result crimes; the most prevalent is criminal homicide.

- Proving causation requires providing two kinds of cause: factual and legal.

- Mistake of fact is a defense when it prevents the formation of the mental attitude required by a criminal statute.

- Ignorance of facts or the law is no defense.

Chapter 4: The General Principles of Criminal Liability—*Mens Rea*, Concurrence, and Causation

KEY TERMS AND CONCEPTS

- **blameworthiness (also called "culpability")**—the idea that we can only punish people that we can blame, and we can only blame people that are responsible for what they do; p. 106

- **cause in fact**—the objective determination that the defendant's act triggered a chain of events that ended as a bad result, such as death in homicide; p. 106, 125

- **legal cause**—a subjective judgment as to whether it's fair and just to blame the defendant for the result; cause recognized by law to impose criminal liability; p. 106, 126

- **principle of *mens rea***—see ***mens rea***; p. 106

- **motive**—the reason why a defendant commits a crime; p. 108

- **subjective fault**—fault that requires a "bad mind" in the actor; p. 109

- **objective fault**—fault that requires no purposeful or conscious "bad mind" in the actor; it sets a standard of what the "average person should have known;" p. 109

- **no fault**—liability that requires neither subjective nor objective fault; p. 110

- **general intent**—intent to commit the *actus reus*—the act required in the definition of the crime; p. 110

- **specific intent**—the attitude represented by subjective fault, where there's a "bad" mind or will that triggers the act; the intent to do something beyond the *actus reus*; p. 110

- **general intent plus**—"general intent" refers to the intent to commit the *actus reus* of the crime; and "plus" refers to some "special mental element," in addition to the intent to commit the criminal act; p. 111

- **purpose (in *mens rea*)**—the specific intent to act and/or cause a criminal harm; p. 113

- **knowledge (in *mens rea*)**—consciously acting or causing a result; p. 116

- **recklessness**—the conscious creation of substantial and unjustifiable risk; p. 117

- **negligence**—the unconscious creation of substantial and unjustifiable risks; p. 118

- **scienter**—the Latin name for "awareness;" p. 116

- **strict liability**—liability without fault, or in the absence of *mens rea;* it's based on voluntary action alone; p. 120

- **principle of concurrence**—some mental fault has to trigger the *actus reus* in criminal conduct crimes and the cause in bad-result crimes; see **concurrence**; p. 123

- **principle of causation**—the requirement that criminal conduct cause a harm defined in the criminal code; p. 124

- **factual ("but for") cause**—conduct that, in fact, leads to a harmful result; p. 124

- **proximate cause**—the main cause of the result of criminal conduct; legal cause; p. 124

- **intervening cause**—the cause that either interrupts a chain of events or substantially contributes to a result; p. 125

- **mistake of fact**—to be mistaken about the law or fact; to believe the facts are one thing when they're really another; a defense whenever the mistake prevents the formation of any fault-based mental attitude; p. 129

- **ignorance of the law**—a defense that the defendant didn't know the rules, so he couldn't know he was breaking the law; p. 129

CHAPTER OUTLINE

I. The Principle of *Mens Rea*

Mens rea is the mental element of a crime that the prosecution must prove beyond a reasonable doubt. There are varying degrees of *mens rea*, and it is possible that a different *mens rea* is required for different elements of the crime (one for the voluntary act, one for the harm, and a different for causation). Thus, *mens rea* law is complicated and somewhat confusing.

A. Serious crimes require both a criminal act (*actus reus*) and criminal intent (*mens rea*).
B. **Proving "State of Mind"**—Proof of *mens rea*
   1. We can't see intent or measure it directly.
   2. We infer intent from actors' actions (circumstantial evidence).
   3. Confessions are the only direct evidence of *mens rea*.
C. **Criminal Intent**—Four kinds of *mens rea* (criminal intent or blameworthy state of mind)
   1. *Mens rea* consists of four states of mind with different levels of culpability.
   2. Motive, although it may or may not be relevant, is not the same thing as *mens rea*. Also, motive may be an element of a crime (for example, the "attendant circumstance" in burglary).
   3. Subjective fault, objective fault, and no-fault liability
      a. Subjective fault requires "bad mind" of the actor.
      b. Objective fault does not require "bad mind" but is present when a reasonable person would have known something that the actor claims he didn't know.
      c. No-fault liability (strict liability) is when the law makes certain behavior a crime, even if the person didn't have any guilty mind.

4. Non-MPC jurisdictions may use the following concepts:
   a. General intent
      (1) Intent to engage in the criminal act
      (2) *Case: Commonwealth v. Gagne*
   b. Specific intent—Sometimes limited to "subjective fault" (see below)
      (1) Intent to cause a specific result; commonly defined as "general intent plus"
      (2) *Case: People v. Disimone*
   c. Transferred intent
   d. Constructive intent
5. **The Model Penal Code's (MPC's) Mental Attitudes**—The four levels of culpability are:
   a. Purpose (or intentionally)—Acting on purpose and/or with the conscious object of causing harm.
      (1) *Case: State v. Stark*
      (2) *Case: Commonwealth v. Barnette*
   b. Knowledge—Acting knowingly but without the conscious purpose or object of causing harm.
      (1) *Case: State v. Jantzi*
   c. Recklessness—Acting with a conscious creation of a high risk of harm.
      (1) *Case: Koppersmith v. State*
   d. Negligence (or criminal negligence)—Acting with an unconscious creation of a high risk of harm.
      (1) *Case: Koppersmith v. State*
D. **Liability without Fault: Strict liability** offenses don't require culpability (i.e., *mens rea*).
   1. Justifications for strict liability
      a. The offenses are a danger to public health, safety, and morals.
      b. Penalties are limited to fines as the only punishment.
   2. Criticisms of strict liability
      a. It violates the basic idea of punishment for culpability.
      b. It could be expanded to include more serious crimes.
   3. *Case: State v. Loge*

II. **The principle of concurrence** states the required relationship between intent and act.
   A. *Mens rea* triggers the criminal act.
   B. Criminal conduct causes the criminal harm.

III. **The principle of causation** states the required relationship between act and harm.
   A. Applies only to crimes of criminal conduct causing criminal harm
   B. Two kinds of causation
      1. **Factual ("but for" or "except for") cause**
         a. Is an empirical question of fact
         b. "Except for" or "but for" an act by the defendant that triggered a chain of events, would this criminal harm have occurred?
         c. A necessary but not sufficient cause for proving causation

2. Legal (proximate) cause
a. Based on a subjective question of fairness: Should the defendant be blamed and punished for this injury or death? Is it fair to hold the defendant responsible?
b. Two types of intervening acts in the chain between the triggering act of the defendant and the criminal harm:
(1) Coincidental intervening acts break the causal chain unless they're predictable or foreseeable.
(2) Responsive intervening acts only break the causal chain if
(a) They're abnormal; or,
(b) They're not predicable or foreseeable.
3. *Case: Commonwealth v. McCloskey*
4. *Case: Velazquez v. State*
5. *Case: People v. Kibbe*
6. *Case: People v. Armitage*

IV. Ignorance and Mistake—Ignorance is not knowing what the facts are; mistakenness is not being correct in what you think you know are the facts or the law.
  A. **Mistake of Fact**—Mistake of fact is generally a defense to a crime; some say it is an excuse, and others say it negates the *mens rea* and there is no liability because all the elements are not present.
   1. Failure of proof of mental element
   2. MPC approach: Mistake matters when it prevents the formation of the specific *mens rea* required by the statute.
   3. Mistake of fact isn't a defense to strict liability crimes.
  B. **Ignorance of the Law**—Is generally not a defense to a crime.
   1. Allowing ignorance of the law as a defense would clash with the principle of legality (see chapter one).

CHAPTER SUMMARY

Most crimes have a *mens rea* or mental element that must be proven by the prosecution beyond a reasonable doubt. The basic idea is that it is not fair to punish someone unless they had some form of mental fault or blameworthiness.

The mental element can apply to or modify other elements of a crime, and thus, a crime can have more than one mental element. For instance, the *mens rea* can apply to the act, the harm, or the circumstances.

General intent means intent to do the criminal act. Specific intent means an intent that applies to any other element of the crime other than the criminal act. Transferred intent is a doctrine that transfers the criminal's intent from the intended victim to the victim the criminal actually hurt.

There are many different types of intent or culpability in various jurisdictions. Many states follow the Model Penal Code approach of having only four types of culpability or *mens rea*: Purpose means it was the actor's conscious object; knowing means that the actor knew something was likely to happen or occur; recklessness means that the person was aware of a serious risk but went ahead and took that risk anyway, even though an objectively reasonable person would not have taken that risk; and negligence means the actor did not conform to the external, objective standard of what a reasonable person would have known or done in the same circumstances. Purpose and knowing are subjective mental states. Recklessness is both objective and subjective. Negligence is a totally objective standard.

A few crimes do not have a *mens rea* element. These are called strict liability crimes and are controversial because they can punish persons who had no mental fault. A person could be punished for an accident. On the other hand, it is argued that certain types of crimes involve important governmental interests and would be too difficult to enforce if a *mens rea* element was required. Strict liability crimes are always minor crimes that are rarely, if ever, punished by imprisonment.

If a crime has a harm or result element, the prosecution must prove that the defendant caused the harm beyond a reasonable doubt. The prosecution must prove that the defendant's acts were both the cause in fact ("but for" cause) and the proximate or legal cause. Cause in fact is an empirical or factual issue. Proximate or legal cause involves the question of whether it is fair or just to make the defendant responsible for a harm that occurred in an unusual fashion. For instance, sometimes a defendant will act and set a chain of events in motion, but some other events will occur after the defendant's act and contribute to causation of the harm. In general, if this intervening cause was normal and foreseeable, the defendant will not be relieved of liability for the harm.

When a person is mistaken as to the fact of something, it may be said that he or she lacks the required mental state about an element of a crime or that they have an excuse defense. Thus, there will generally be no criminal liability in the case of a mistaken fact. But, when a person is mistaken as to what the law provides about a certain conduct, they may not avoid criminal liability because criminal laws can't be ignored or contradicted by allowing defendants to plead that their ignorance excuses their behavior.

Study Guide

PRACTICE TEST BANK

MULTIPLE CHOICE

1. The mental element of a crime is called the _____.

    a. *actus reus*
    b. *mens rea*
    c. harm
    d. concurrence

2. In the absence of a confession, intent must generally be proven by _____ evidence.

    a. peremptory
    b. exclusive
    c. referential
    d. circumstantial

3. General intent is the intent to _____.

    a. do a criminal act
    b. cause a result
    c. cause the circumstances
    d. have the *mens rea*

4. John received a slingshot for his birthday. He wanted to practice his shot, and so he went out into the crowded sheets and let a stone fly. Although he didn't intend to hit any of the many people he saw, it hit Jill in the forehead and caused her death. John acted _____.

    a. intentionally
    b. knowingly
    c. recklessly
    d. negligently

5 A *mens rea* requirement that applies to anything other than the *actus reus* is called _____ intent.

    a. strict
    b. specific
    c. transferred
    d. general

6. The objective reasonable person standard is used in the definition of _____.

   a. negligence
   b. purposely
   c. knowingly
   d. transferred intent

7. The strongest objection to strict liability laws is that _____.

   a. they result in the punishment of people who are not blameworthy
   b. long periods of imprisonment are authorized for such offenses
   c. there is no strong public interest in preventing these crimes
   d. conviction of such offenses carries a heavy stigma equivalent to burglary or robbery

8. In the case of *State v. Stark,* the court held that Stark acted _____ in exposing several women to HIV.

   a. recklessly
   b. knowingly
   c. accidentally
   d. negligently

9. A defendant is criminally responsible for harm if the defendant's conduct was the _____.

   a. cause in fact and proximate cause
   b. "but for" cause of the harm
   c. natural result of the conduct
   d. intervening cause

10. *Mens rea* elements _____.

    a. apply only to the act element
    b. apply only to the harm element
    c. can apply to other *mens rea* elements
    d. can apply to any other element except *mens rea*

11. Which of the following is not a type of culpability in the Model Penal Code?

    a. purpose
    b. knowledge
    c. intention
    d. negligence

12. If it is not the defendant's conscious objective to cause the harm, but he is aware that the harm will occur, the defendant is said to have the *mens rea* termed _____.

    a. knowledge
    b. consciousness
    c. awareness
    d. complicity

13. Conscious risk creation is referred to as _____.

    a. purpose
    b. negligence
    c. recklessness
    d. perspicacity

14. If an actor does not behave like an objectively reasonable person would have under the same circumstances, the actor is _____.

    a. reckless
    b. feckless
    c. wanton
    d. negligent

15. Which of the following types of culpability is both objective and subjective?

    a. negligent
    b. reckless
    c. knowing
    d. purpose

16. Absence of knowledge about the facts surrounding an issue is called _____.

    a. mistake of fact
    b. ignorance of facts
    c. mistake of law
    d. ignorance of law

17. Factual cause is also referred to as a _____ cause.

    a. legal
    b. proximate
    c. but for
    d. distal

18. An event that occurs between the defendant's act and the harm and has a causal connection to the harm is called a/n _____ act or cause.

    a. intervening
    b. concurrent
    c. consecutive
    d. contingent

19. The prosecution must prove that the defendant caused the harm _____.

    a. by a preponderance of the evidence
    b. beyond a moral certainty
    c. by clear and convincing evidence
    d. beyond a reasonable doubt

20. One definition of the term "concurrence" requires that the criminal intent _____.

    a. cause the act
    b. cause the harm
    c. cause the *mens rea*
    d. be the proximate cause of the circumstances

21. A bartender serves 18-year-old Jim a beer thinking he is 21. Jim had produced a very professional looking fake identification. If the state has a statute saying that it is a crime to intentionally or knowingly serve anyone under 21 alcohol, the bartender will most likely be found _____.

    a. not guilty due to mistake of fact
    b. guilty because the crime is a strict liability crime
    c. guilty because the mistake of fact wasn't reasonable
    d. not guilty due to ignorance of the law

22. In the Model Penal Code, the most blameworthy state of mind is _____.

    a. recklessness
    b. negligent
    c. purpose
    d. intention

23. An accidental injury can be a crime if the criminal statute is of the _____ type.

    a. strict liability
    b. capital
    c. vicarious liability
    d. mendacious

24. "But for" causation can also be referred to as "_____ for" causation.

    a. except
    b. in lieu
    c. and
    d. contingent

25. Legal or proximate cause issues involve the _____.

    a. empirical connection between the act and harm
    b. "but for" test
    c. "except for" test
    d. justice of making the defendant responsible for this harm

26. If a responsive, intervening act is normal and foreseeable, the defendant _____.

    a. is not responsible for the harm
    b. is responsible only for negligent offenses
    c. is responsible only for reckless harms
    d. is responsible for the harm

27. Mistake of fact cuts off liability to the actor because it is viewed as _____.

    a. a defense of excuse
    b. having the absence of a *mens rea*
    c. both a defense of excuse and the absence of *mens rea*
    d. neither a defense of excuse nor the absence of *mens rea*

28. A criminal statute is more likely to have more than one _____ element than it is to have more than one element of any other kind.

    a. intent
    b. act
    c. cause
    d. concurrence

29. U.S. Supreme Court Justice Oliver Wendell Holmes' statement that even a dog can distinguish between a kick and being stumbled over, highlights the importance of the _____ element of crimes.

    a. harm
    b. result
    c. concurrence
    d. intent

30. Being aware of a serious risk but taking it anyway is the form of intent termed _____.

    a. negligence
    b. recklessness
    c. knowledge
    d. purpose

TRUE/FALSE

1. In the absence of a confession, *mens rea* is usually proven by circumstantial evidence.
    a. true
    b. false

2. Different kinds of intent indicate different levels of blameworthiness.
    a. true
    b. false

3. Specific intent is intent to do the criminal act.
    a. true
    b. false

4. The four levels of culpability or intent in the Model Penal Code are purpose, knowledge, recklessness, and negligence.
    a. true
    b. false

5. Negligence is the most blameworthy form of intent.
    a. true
    b. false

6. Recklessness requires awareness of substantial and unjustifiable risks.
    a. true
    b. false

7. Negligence has both an objective and subjective component.
    a. true
    b. false

8. Strict liability crimes have no *actus reus* element.
    a. true
    b. false

9. In strict liability crimes, accidental injury can be criminal.
    a. true
    b. false

10. Proving criminal causation requires proving both factual and legal cause.
    a. true
    b. false

11. Intervening causes can never be proximate causes.
    a. true
    b. false

12. Specific intent is intent that is transferred to another victim.
    a. true
    b. false

13. The most blameworthy state of mind in the Model Penal Code is purpose.
    a. true
    b. false

14. Negligence involves conscious risk creation.
    a. true
    b. false

15. The issue of factual cause involves the "but for" test.
    a. true
    b. false

16. Negligence is a totally objective standard.
    a. true
    b. false

17. Questions of fairness and justice figure into the factual cause determination.
    a. true
    b. false

18. Factual cause is an empirical question.
    a. true
    b. false

19. A normal, foreseeable responsive intervening act will not prevent criminal liability for a crime.
    a. true
    b. false

20. An abnormal and unforeseeable intervening cause will generally not relieve the defendant of liability for causing the harm.
    a. true
    b. false

21. An earthquake could be an intervening cause.
    a. true
    b. false

22. Strict liability crimes always violate due process.
    a. true
    b. false

23. Premeditation, wickedly, and designedly are all example of *mens rea*.
    a. true
    b. false

24. A person can't evade liability by claiming mistake of fact to a strict liability crime.
    a. true
    b. false

25. The burden of proof on the causation issue is on the defendant.
    a. true
    b. false

FILL-IN-THE-BLANK

1. The "except for" test is better known as the "_____" test.

2. Fairness and justice come into play in the legal or _____ test of causation.

3. The form of intent involving having a conscious objective is _____.

4. Negligence is a totally _____ standard.

5. _____ involves conscious risk creation.

6. _____ is intent to do the criminal act.

7. The mental element of the crime is called the _____.

8. _____ evidence proves a fact indirectly or by inference.

9. _____ is intent that applies to elements other than the act.

10. _____ is a defense to a crime if it prevents the formation of a culpable state of mind.

11. Absence of knowledge about what the law states is called _____.

12. A crime without an intent element is called a _____ crime.

13. The most blameworthy form of intent in the Model Penal Code is _____.

14. The least blameworthy form of intent in the Model Penal Code is _____.

15. Proximate cause is also referred to as _____.

ESSAY

1. Compare and contrast specific and general intent. Be sure to provide examples.

2. Define and discuss strict liability crimes. What is the justification for such crimes? Be sure to provide examples.

3. What does the criminal law require in the way of a relationship between the act and intent? Why is this relationship important? Be sure to provide examples.

4. Compare and contrast factual causation and legal causation. Why must the defendant be both the factual and legal/proximate cause of the harm in order for him to have liability? When will intervening variables cut off liability? Give examples.

5. List and define the four types of *mens rea* found in the Model Penal Code. Define each and give an example.

CHAPTER 4 ANSWER KEY

Multiple Choice

1. b	2. d	3. a	4. c	5. b
6. a	7. a	8. b	9. a	10. d
11. c	12. a	13. c	14. d	15. b
16. b	17. c	18. a	19. d	20. a
21. a	22. c	23. a	24. a	25. d
26. d	27. c	28. a	29. d	30. b

True/False

1. T	2. T	3. F	4. T	5. F
6. T	7. F	8. F	9. T	10. T
11. F	12. F	13. T	14. F	15. T
16. T	17. F	18. T	19. T	20. F
21. T	22. F	23. T	24. T	25. F

Fill-in-the-Blank

1. but for
2. proximate
3. purpose
4. objective
5. Recklessness
6. general intent
7. *mens rea*
8. circumstantial
9. specific intent
10. mistake of fact
11. ignorance of the law
12. strict liability
13. purpose
14. negligence
15. legal cause

CHAPTER 5
DEFENSES TO CRIMINAL LIABILITY: JUSTIFICATIONS

LEARNING OBJECTIVES

After studying this chapter, students will understand that:

- Defendants who plead justification admit they're responsible for committing crimes but contend they're right under the circumstances.

- Defendants who plead excuse admit they're wrong but contend that, under the circumstances, they're not responsible.

- The heart of self-defense is necessity.

- Use of deadly force in self-defense is limited to preventing imminent death or serious bodily injury to yourself or others.

- There's no duty to retreat from your own home if retreating threatens your personal safety.

- The right to defend your home sometimes includes the right to use deadly force.

- The choice-of-evils defense justifies choosing to commit a lesser crime to avoid an imminent threat of harm from a greater crime.

- The heart of the defense of consent is the high value placed on individual autonomy in a free society.

KEY TERMS AND CONCEPTS

- **justification** defenses—defendants admit they were responsible for their acts but claim what they did was right (justified) under the circumstances; p. 138

- **excuses defenses**—defendants admit what they did was *wrong* but claim that under the circumstances, they weren't *responsible* for what they did; p. 138

- **affirmative defense**—defense in which the defendant bears the burden of production; p.138

- **burden of production**—the responsibility to introduce initial evidence to support a defense; p. 139

- **burden of persuasion**—the responsibility to convince the fact finder of the truth of the defense; p. 139

- **preponderance of the evidence**—more than 50 percent of the evidence proves justification or excuse; p. 139

- **perfect defenses**—defenses that lead to outright acquittal; p. 139

- **imperfect defenses**—defenses reducing, but not eliminating, criminal liability; p. 139

- **necessity**—general principle of an honest and reasonable belief; p. 140

- **initial aggressor**—someone who provokes an attack and therefore can't use force to defend himself against the attack provoked; p. 140

- **withdrawal exception**—if initial aggressors completely withdraw from the fights they provoke, they can claim the defense of self-defense; p. 140

- **imminent danger**—element in self-defense that injury or death is going to happen right now; p. 141

- **present danger**—danger that's probably going to happen some time in the future but not right now (self-defense); p. 145

- **retreat rule**—you have to retreat but only if you reasonably believe that backing off won't unreasonably put you in danger of death or serious bodily harm; p. 150

- **stand-your-ground rule**—if you didn't start the fight, you can stand your ground and kill; p. 150

- **curtilage**—the area immediately surrounding a dwelling; p. 154

- **necessity (choice-of-evils defense)**—general principle of an honest and reasonable belief that it's necessary to commit a lesser crime (evil) to prevent the imminent danger of a greater crime (evil); p. 158

- **general principle of necessity (defense to crime)**—the justification of committing a lesser crime to avoid the imminent danger of a greater crime; p. 158

- **defense of consent**—a justification defense that says if mentally competent adults want to be crime victims, no paternalistic government should get in their way; p. 163

CHAPTER OUTLINE

I. Types of Defenses
    A. There are three legitimate types:
        1. Alibi—defendant proves it was impossible for him to have committed the crime because defendant was elsewhere.
        2. Justification—defendant responsible, but the act was justified.
        3. Excuse—defendant did it, but isn't responsible for his action.
    B. **Affirmative Defenses and Proving Them**
        1. In some jurisdictions, defendants have some responsibility to prove their affirmative defenses.
        2. In other jurisdictions, the government has some responsibility to disprove such defenses.
    C. Results of defendants' successful proof of defense
        1. Perfect defenses—an acquittal results.
        2. Imperfect defenses—reduce the crime to a lesser offense.
        3. Mitigating circumstances—reduce the penalty for the crime.
    D. Motive can be an element and/or influence punishment.

II. **Self-Defense**—Self-defense is a justification for the use of force.
    A. **Elements**
        1. **Unprovoked Attack**
            a. Self-defense not available to initial aggressor.
            b. Total withdrawal by attacker an exception
        2. **Imminent Danger, Necessity, and Reasonable Force**
            a. Honest and reasonable belief in imminent danger of death or serious bodily injury
            b. Reasonable (not excessive) force to repel attack
            c. *Case: People v. Goetz*
        3. **Present Danger**
            a. Honest and reasonable belief in the need to defend against attack right now—imminent or present danger
            b. *Case: State v. Stewart*
            c. *Case: State v. Hundley*
    B. The **retreat** doctrine may limit self-defense.
        1. Two rules
            a. Retreat rule: you have to retreat if escape is reasonable (most states).
            b. Stand your ground rule: if you didn't start the fight, you can stand your ground even if you could escape by retreating (a few states).
        2. Castle exception—retreat from/in home not required; you can stand your ground.
        3. Case: U.S. v. Peterson
        4. Case: State v. Quarles

Chapter 5: Defenses to Criminal Liability—Justifications

III. Defense of Others—The defense of others is a justification for the use of force.
    A. Who is included?
        1. Most states include individuals in a "special relationship."
        2. Some states include anyone in imminent danger of harm.
    B. Defense applies only to those who can claim the right to defend themselves.

IV. In the Defense of Home and Property—The defense of home and property is a justification for the use of force.
    A. Rooted in ancient idea that our home is our castle
    B. Extension of the right of self-defense
    C. Limits to using deadly force vary by state.
        1. Must have reasonable belief intruders intend to commit:
            a. Violent felonies against occupants
            b. Any felony
            c. Any offense
        2. Area covered
            a. Entry into occupied home
            b. Entry into curtilage
    D. *Case: Law v. State*
    E. *Case: People v. Guenther*

V. Necessity ("Choice-of-Evils")—The choice-of-evils defense is a justification defense.
    A. Basic idea—Immediate necessity justifies choosing to commit a lesser crime to avoid the harm of a greater crime.
    B. Elements
        1. Identify evils (usually in legislation)
        2. Rank evils (usually in legislation)
        3. Choose the lesser evil to avoid imminent harm from the greater evil.
    C. *Case: The Queen v. Dudley and Stephens*
    D. *Case: U.S. v. Aguilar et. al*
    E. *Case: State v. Ownby*
    F. *Case: People v. Dover*
    G. *Case: State v. Celli*

VI. Consent—The defense of consent is a justification for some crimes.
    A. Justification—the value of individual autonomy in a free society
    B. Consent is not a defense, but there are four exceptions.
        1. No serious injury results from consent.
        2. Injury occurs during sporting events.
        3. Consent benefits the person who consents (patient consents to surgery).
        4. Consent is a defense to certain sex crimes.
    C. Exceptions are necessary to the defense but are not enough unless consent is also voluntary and knowing.
    D. *Case: State v. Shelley*
    E. *Case: State v, Hiott*
    F. *Case: State v. Brown*
    G. *Case: State v. Fransua*

CHAPTER SUMMARY

There are three kinds of defenses: alibis, justifications, and excuses. Alibis free defendants from criminal liability, because they prove it's impossible for the defendants to have committed the crime because they were somewhere else at the time of the crime. Justifications free defendants from criminal liability, because they prove the defendants aren't blameworthy. Their criminal acts were right or justified. An example is self-defense, which excuses free defendants from criminal liability, because they prove the defendants aren't responsible for their acts. An example is the insanity defense.

All the justification defenses are exceptions to the rule of law. They allow individuals to take the law into their own hands. According to the rule of law, the government has a monopoly on the use of force. Use of force by individuals must be justified by law.

Self-defense is a concession to necessity and is only justified when the force is reasonably and immediately necessary for defense. Deadly force is justified only when the necessity is unprovoked and the attack involves threatened death or serious bodily injury. The amount of force used must be the minimum amount reasonably necessary to defend against an imminent threat. The general rule is that a person must retreat if they can safely do so before using deadly force. This rule puts a premium on human life—even the life of an attacker. The castle exception, and the rules regarding the defense of home, clearly demonstrate that the ancient doctrine that homes are castles is still alive and well. In general, a person is not required to retreat from or in their own home before using deadly force.

The right to defend others includes everyone from close family members to any stranger who needs immediate protection from attack. The same rules apply in self-defense.

The choice-of-evils defense is also based on necessity. This defense protects those who make the right choice in deciding to commit a lesser crime to avoid the imminent harm of a greater crime or social harm. The crime results in a net social good.

The general rule is that consent by the victim is not a defense. However, consent is a defense to some crimes in some circumstances. The consent must be knowing and voluntary. The value of individual autonomy (not necessity) is the heart of the defense of consent.

PRACTICE TEST BANK

MULTIPLE CHOICE

1. Which of the following is not one of the three types of legal defenses to crime?

    a. alibi
    b. justifications
    c. excuses
    d. mitigating circumstances

2. The current approach to self-defense requires that the defender _____.

    a. ward off future attacks by using a preemptive strike
    b. reasonably believe in the danger of an imminent attack
    c. use whatever amount of force the defender subjectively thinks is justified
    d. provoked the incident

3. In justification defenses, defendants admit they did the act but seek acquittal on the ground that their acts _____.

    a. were right
    b. were wrong, but they shouldn't be held responsible
    c. were not done purposely
    d. were done accidentally

4. The amount of force that the law allows to be used in self-defense is the minimum amount _____.

    a. reasonably excessive
    b. reasonably necessary
    c. unreasonably sufficient
    d. inversely proportionate

5. Under the castle exception to the retreat doctrine, the defender does not have to retreat before using defensive force if they _____.

    a. were the initial aggressor
    b. were verbally provoked by the attacker
    c. are attacked in their own home
    d. have already retreated once

6. The choice-of-evils defense is also known as the _____.

    a. public duty defense
    b. rational behavior defense
    c principle or defense of necessity
    d. rational person test

7. In general, consent is _____.

    a. not a defense to crime
    b. a defense only to crimes resulting in death or serious bodily injury
    c. not a defense to intentional or purposeful crime
    d. a defense only if the conduct that causes injury has no benefit to society

8. The most famous English case involving choice-of-evils defense was _____.

    a. *The Queen v. Dunn and Bradstreet*
    b. *The Queen v. Bradley and Clemens*
    c. *The Queen v. Cooper and Lybrands*
    d. *The Queen v. Dudley and Stephens*

9. The reason why a person commits a crime is called _____.

    a. the motive
    b. the *mens rea*
    c. an excuse
    d. a justification

10 A consent defense to a charge of assault is most likely to succeed when _____.

    a. the assaulter is weaker and smaller than the victim
    b. the assault occurs in a lawful sporting event
    c. the victim is already injured
    d. the consent is given after the assault

11. In order for the consent of the victim to be a valid defense, the consent must be _____.

    a. knowing and subjective
    b. voluntary and objective
    c. in writing
    d. voluntary and knowing

12. Which of the following is a step in the Model Penal Code approach to the choice-of-evils defense?

    a. compare the possible sentences for the two crimes involved
    b. rank the culpability involved in the two offenses at issue
    c. rank the harms
    d. choose the greater evil to avoid the lesser evil

13. To have a valid claim of using force to defend another person, the defendant must show that _____.

    a. the attacker also threatened to use force against the defender
    b. the person defended had a right to use force to defend themselves
    c. the use of force by the attacker against the victim was lawful
    d. the defender must be stronger than the person attacked

14. In *State v. Stewart*, Mrs. Stewart killed her husband while he was asleep. She argued self-defense. On appeal, the court concluded that Mrs. Stewart _____.

    a. did not act in self-defense because she failed to prove that she suffered from battered woman syndrome
    b. was not entitled to the defense because she had other options besides killing
    c. was not entitled to defend herself because she used deadly force
    d. did not act in self-defense because the threat to her from her husband was not imminent

15. One of the most controversial self-defense cases of the 1980s occurred in the New York subway. The defendant was _____.

    a. Troy Canty
    b. Barry Allen
    c. Darrell Caby
    d. Bernhard Goetz

16. The party that has the burden of persuasion on an issue must _____.

    a. prove the point or lose on the issue
    b. present some evidence to get the issue into the case
    c. inform the jury before trial that they will raise the issue
    d. present enough evidence to meet the burden of production

17. The appellate court in *State v. Shelly* and the Model Penal Code limit the use of the consent defense to sporting activities where the injury and conduct are _____.

    a. reasonably foreseeable hazards
    b. a felony offense
    c. specifically agreed to before the contest begins
    d. permitted by the rules of the game

18. Nearly all states allow the use of deadly force in some circumstances to _____.

    a. resist a lawful arrest
    b. protect their home
    c. stop a person committing any type of misdemeanor in the home
    d. stop a person from committing a felony in a public place

19. A defense in which defendants admit the act but claim they aren't legally responsible is called a/n _____.

    a. justification
    b. claim of right
    c. mitigating condition
    d. excuse

20. If the defendant establishes a perfect defense, the defendant _____.

    a. is committed to a mental hospital
    b. may still be convicted of a lesser offense
    c. is entitled to be found not guilty
    d. is entitled to a reduced sentence

21. A defendant is charged with murder but manages to get a conviction on manslaughter. This can occur if a defendant establishes certain types of _____.

    a. justifications
    b. excuses
    c. mitigating circumstances
    d. imperfect defenses

22. A person who violates the speed limit in order to get a critically injured person to the emergency room may claim which of the following defenses?

    a. duress
    b. necessity
    c. coercion
    d. statute of limitations

23. In most jurisdictions, the defendant's belief that self-defense was necessary must be sincere and _____.

    a. objectively reasonable
    b. subjectively unreasonable
    c. empirically accurate
    d. empirically verifiable

24. Defensive force may be used lawfully only if the danger is _____.

    a. foreseeable
    b. imminent
    c. mandatory
    d. contingent

25. The general rule is that self-defense is lawfully available only against ____ attacks.

    a. unprovoked
    b. justified
    c. legal
    d. excusable

26. Persons who are the initial, unprovoked aggressor can acquire a lawful right to defend themselves if they _____ from the fight they started.

    a. clearly desist
    b. irrevocably renounce themselves
    c. contingently abstain
    d. completely withdraw

27. The true man rule for retreat before using force is also known as the _____ rule.

    a. castle
    b. stand-your-ground
    c. reasonable retreat
    d. foreseeable desistance

28. A defense which requires the defendant to produce some evidence of the defense before the jury will be allowed to consider the defense is a/n _____.

    a. imperfect defense
    b. perfect defense
    c. statutory defense
    d. affirmative defense

29. Circumstances about the crime that may reduce the punishment are called _____ circumstances.

    a. contingent
    b. foreseeable
    c. mitigating
    d. compensatory

30. Justifications focus on the _____.

    a. personal accountability of the defendant
    b. the rightfulness of an otherwise criminal act
    c. legal responsibility of the defendant
    d. mitigating circumstances

TRUE/FALSE

1. A perfect defense leads to an acquittal.
    a. true
    b. false

2. It is never lawful to use force to protect property.
    a. true
    b. false

3. Preemptive strikes at a potential attacker are valid self-defense.
    a. true
    b. false

4. Consent is never a defense to any sex crime.
    a. true
    b. false

5. The term "motive" means the same as "intent."
    a. true
    b. false

6. In the alibi defense, defendants argue that they were somewhere other at the time of the crime and not at the scene of the crime.
    a. true
    b. false

7. Retaliation for past attacks or threats justifies defensive use of force.
    a. true
    b. false

8. There is no defense for using force against someone who is not attacking the actor but is attacking some other person.
   a. true
   b. false

9. Defendants prove most defenses beyond a reasonable doubt.
   a. true
   b. false

10. If the convicted defendant shows mitigating circumstances, they may be able to get a reduced sentence.
    a. true
    b. false

11. Necessity or choice-of-evils is not a valid defense if the state has already ranked the evils and specifically precluded the choice, such as the use of marijuana to alleviate pain.
    a. true
    b. false

12. In both excuses and justifications, the defendant admits doing the *actus reus*.
    a. true
    b. false

13. The burden of production is on the defendant for affirmative defenses.
    a. true
    b. false

14. Imperfect self-defense may, in some jurisdictions, reduce a murder to manslaughter.
    a. true
    b. false

15. The reason why the person commits the crime is called the motive.
    a. true
    b. false

16. In all states, a person must retreat from their home if they can safely do so before using deadly force.
    a. true
    b. false

17. A person cannot lawfully use force to prevent an anticipated attack.
    a. true
    b. false

Study Guide

18. No matter what may happen later, the initial attacker can never claim self-defense.
   a. true
   b. false

19. The Model Penal Code recognizes a choice-of-evils defense.
   a. true
   b. false

20. The choice-of-evils defense requires that the defendant have correctly identified and weighed the evils.
   a. true
   b. false

21. The choice-of-evils defense was available at common law.
   a. true
   b. false

22. The outside area immediately surrounding the home is called the curtilage.
   a. true
   b. false

23. At common law, the right to use deadly force to defend your own home was not recognized.
   a. true
   b. false

24. In many jurisdictions, deadly force can be used to defend yourself against certain serious felonies.
   a. true
   b. false

25. Consent is a defense to all crimes.
   a. true
   b. false

FILL-IN-THE-BLANK

1. Only the danger of a/n _____ attack justifies the use of force in self-defense.

2. Under the _____ exception to the retreat doctrine, one does not have to retreat in one's own home before using defensive force.

3. To have a valid claim of self-defense, the actor must have had an honest and _____ belief in the necessity of using force.

4. _____ is danger that a person reasonably believes is always hanging over them.

5. The law regarding defense of homes is influenced by the common-law idea that a person's home is their _____.

6. The criminal law generally excludes the defense of _____, where serious injury is inflicted on the victim.

7. Running a stop sign to get a seriously ill person to the hospital would be an example of the _____ defense.

8. A/n _____ defense is one that reduces, but does not eliminate, criminal liability.

9. The duty to retreat before using deadly force is weakest when the person is attacked in their _____.

10. The lawn and/or other space immediately outside the home is called the _____.

11. The _____ is the reason for committing crime.

12. _____ circumstances are circumstances which may lead to a reduction in sentence.

13. The true man rule is also known as the _____ rule.

14. A/n _____ defense is one that, if established, requires a verdict of not guilty.

15. The burden of proof or _____ is a party's obligation to finally prove (or disprove) a defense or other matter.

ESSAY

1. Define, describe, compare, and contrast justifications and excuses. Give examples. What role does the defendant play in raising the defenses of justification and excuse? Do defenses always get the defendant off?

2. Discuss the defense of consent. Be sure to provide examples.

3. Discuss fully the choice-of-evils defense and present an example of where the defense would be valid and another example where it would not be valid.

4. Discuss the general rules on the use of force, deadly force, and retreat. Be sure to provide examples.

5. Discuss the use of force in defense of home and property. Why does the law generally disallow the use of deadly force to defend home and property unless certain circumstances exist?

CHAPTER 5 ANSWER KEY

Multiple Choice

1. d	2. b	3. a	4. b	5. c
6. c	7. a	8. d	9. a	10. b
11. d	12. b	13. b	14. d	15. d
16. d	17. a	18. b	19. d	20. c
21. d	22. b	23. a	24. b	25. a
26. d	27. b	28. d	29. c	30. b

True/False

1. T	2. F	3. F	4. F	5. F
6. T	7. F	8. F	9. F	10. T
11. T	12. T	13. T	14. T	15. T
16. F	17. T	18. F	19. T	20. T
21. T	22. T	23. F	24. T	25. F

Fill-in-the-Blank

1. imminent
2. castle
3. reasonable
4. Present danger
5. castle
6. consent
7. choice-of-evils
8. imperfect
9. home
10. curtilage
11. motive
12. Mitigating
13. stand-your-ground
14. perfect
15. persuasion

CHAPTER 6
DEFENSES TO CRIMINAL LIABILITY: EXCUSES

LEARNING OBJECTIVES

After studying this chapter, students will understand that:

- Defendants who plead an excuse defense admit what they did was wrong but argue that, under the circumstances, they weren't responsible for their actions.

- The defense of insanity excuses criminal liability when it seriously damages defendants' capacity to control their acts and/or capacity to reason and understand the wrongfulness of their conduct.

- Few defendants plead the insanity defense, and those who do rarely succeed.

- Insanity isn't the equivalent of mental disease or defect.

- The right-wrong test focuses on defects in reason or cognition.

- The volitional incapacity test focuses on defects in self-control or will.

- The substantial capacity test focuses on reason *and* self-control.

- The product-of-mental-illness test focuses on criminal acts resulting from mental disease.

- Current trends favor shifting the burden of proof for insanity to defendants.

- Diminished capacity and diminished responsibility apply only to homicide.

- Juvenile court judges can use their discretion to transfer a juvenile to adult criminal court.

- It's sometimes OK to excuse people who harm innocent people to save themselves.

- Voluntary intoxication is no excuse for committing a crime; involuntary intoxication is.

- Entrapment is used in all societies, even though it violates a basic purpose of government in free societies—to prevent crime, not to encourage it.

- Despite the immense criticism of them, syndrome excuses should be taken seriously.

KEY TERMS AND CONCEPTS

failure-of-proof theory—the defendant disproves the prosecution's case by showing he or she couldn't have formed the state of mind required to prove the mental element of the crime; p. 174

insanity—a legal term for a person who is excused from criminal liability because a mental disease or defect impairs his or her *mens rea*; p. 175

civil commitment—involuntary confinement not based on criminal conviction; p. 175

right-wrong test (*M'Naghten* rule)—test used in insanity defense to determine the defendant's capacity to either know right from wrong or to know the act is against the law; p. 177

irresistible impulse test—tests whether the will is so impaired that it makes it impossible for the person to control the impulse to do wrong; p. 181

substantial capacity test—insanity due to mental disease or defect impairing the substantial capacity either to appreciate the wrongfulness of conduct or to conform behavior to the law; p. 182

product-of-mental-illness test—a test to determine whether a crime was a product of mental disease or defect; p. 186

diminished capacity—mental capacity less than "normal" but more than "insane;" an attempt to prove that the defendant, incapable of the requisite intent of the crime charged, is innocent of that crime but may well be guilty of a lesser one; p. 187

diminished responsibility—a defense of excuse in which the defendant argues, "What I did was wrong, but under the circumstances I'm *less* responsible;" p. 187

judicial waiver—when a juvenile court judge uses their discretion to transfer a juvenile to adult criminal court; p. 189

defense of duress—the excuse of being forced to commit a crime; p. 191

entrapment—government actions that induce individuals to commit crimes that they otherwise wouldn't commit; p. 194

subjective test of entrapment—focuses on the predisposition of defendants to commit crimes; p. 195

objective test of entrapment—focuses on the actions that government agents take to induce individuals to commit crimes; p. 198

syndrome—novel defenses of excuse based on symptoms of conditions, such as being a Vietnam vet suffering from post-traumatic stress disorder or having premenstrual symptoms; p. 198

CHAPTER OUTLINE

I. Excuses are a form of defense to a criminal charge.
    A. Difference between justification and excuse
        1. Justification—admits responsibility, but, under the circumstances, claims it was the right thing
        2. Excuse—admits doing wrong but, under the circumstances, claims not legally responsible

II. **Insanity**—Insanity is a defense based on a defendant's mental disease or defect.
    A. Definition—The defendant was so mentally diseased, he couldn't know nature of acts or control actions.
    B. A legal, but not a medical, concept
    C. Rationale—can't blame people who aren't responsible
    D. Consequence—civil commitment, not freedom
    E. **The Right-Wrong Test**
        1. Right-wrong test elements
            a. Mental disease (psychosis) or defect (retardation) damaged reason at the time of the crime.
            b. The defendant didn't know (simple awareness).
                (1) Nature of actions
                (2) Right or wrong
                      (a) Legal wrong
                      (b) Moral wrong
        2. *Case: State v. Odell*
    F. **The Irresistible Impulse Test**
        1. Irresistible impulse test elements
            a. The defendant had a mental disease or defect at the time of the crime.
            b. The defendant knew the nature of the act and knew it was wrong.
            c. The mental disease or defect caused an impulse he couldn't control (volitional failure).
    G. **The Substantial Capacity Test**
        1. Substantial capacity test elements (Model Penal Code)
            a. The mental disease or defect damages either or both reason and will.
            b. The mental disease or defect causes
                (1) Substantial (not complete) lack of reason and control
                (2) Failure to appreciate (not just purely intellectual awareness of) nature or wrongfulness
                (3) Failure to conform behavior to law
        2. *Case: People v. Drew*

Chapter 6: Defenses to Criminal Liability—Excuses

H. **The Product-of-Mental-Illness Test**
    1. Product-of-mental-illness test elements (Durham rule)
        a. Checks for both reason and will
        b. Acts that are a product of mental illness excuse criminal liability.
I. The Burden of Proof
    1. States vary as to who has to prove insanity and to what level of certainty.
        a. Federal law prior to the Hinckley case, for example, required government to prove the defendant was not insane to beyond a reasonable doubt.
        b. Federal law after the Hinckley case, requires defendants to prove they were insane by clear and convincing evidence.

III. **Diminished Capacity**—The diminished capacity defense negates intent.
    A. Mental disease or defect diminishes capacity but not enough to qualify as insanity defense.
    B. Limited to diseases or defects that make it impossible to form the intent required to commit the crime.

IV. **Age**—Age is a defense or a basis for juvenile court jurisdiction.
    A. Immaturity excuses criminal liability, but statutes vary as to the age of capacity.
    B. Age of maturity varies, but three stages at common law and later:
        1) Early childhood—can't form criminal intent (irrebuttable presumption)
        2) Middle childhood—refutable presumption against capacity to form intent
        3) Adult—conclusive presumption of capacity to form intent
    C. Age can aggravate as well as excuse criminal responsibility.
    D. Age of capacity is different than the jurisdiction of the courts to try young offenders. Young offenders in all jurisdictions may be subject to the jurisdiction of juvenile courts for certain offenses. Youthful offenders may also be waived into adult courts.
        1) Judicial waivers
        2) Prosecutorial waivers
        3) Legislative waivers
    E. *Case: State v. K.R.L.*

V. **Duress**
    A. **The Problem of Duress**
        1. Duress is a defense involving a person being threatened if they don't commit a crime.
        2. Should we excuse those who hurt others to save themselves?
    B. **The Elements of Duress**
        1. Threats amounting to duress: kinds of threats vary from killing to doing serious bodily harm
        2. Immediacy of the threats: from instant to imminent threat
        3. Crimes the defense applies to qualifying crimes vary from minor to serious (never for homicide).
        4. Degree of belief regarding the threat: measurement of belief regarding threats varies as to objective or subjective.

VI. Intoxication—Intoxication may or may not be a defense.
    A. Conflicting principles of accountability and causation
    B. Voluntary is no excuse; involuntary is an excuse.
    C. Statutes may provide that voluntary intoxication, which negates a *mens rea* element of a crime, may reduce culpability.

VII. Entrapment is a defense based on the conduct of the police.
    A. Definition—police inducting someone to commit a crime they wouldn't otherwise commit
    B. Defense of entrapment is not of constitutional origin.
    C. **The Subjective Test**—majority rule
        1. Did criminal intent originate with the government?
        2. Was the defendant predisposed to commit the crime?
        3. *Case: Oliver v. State*
        4. *Case: De Pasquale v. State*
        5. *Case: U.S. v. Simpson*
    D. **The Objective Test**—minority rule
        1. Did criminal intent originate with the government?
        2. Would ordinary (reasonable), law-abiding people be tempted to commit the crime?
        3. Dismiss even if the defendant is predisposed.

VIII. Syndromes—Syndrome defenses involve a variety of mental conditions.
    A. Groups of symptoms (syndromes) impair mental capacity
    B. Affects defendant's capacity to form specific intent
    C. Expert testimony is used to inform the jury of the syndrome.
    D. *Case: State v. Phipps*

CHAPTER SUMMARY

Defendants who plead excuses admit what they did was wrong but claim they weren't responsible because of mental abnormality or unusual circumstances.

The excuse of insanity is rarely used, rarely successful, and almost always leads to at least temporary civil commitment if successful. The defense of insanity stands for the proposition that we can't blame people who aren't responsible because of mental diseases or defects that impair their reason or will. Insanity is not the equivalent of mental disease or defect; rather, it is caused by mental disease or defect.

There are a number of tests of the insanity defense. The right-wrong (M'Naghten) test focuses on defects in reason. The product-of-mental-illness test (Durham rule) focuses on criminal acts resulting from (are the product of) mental disease. The irresistible impulse test focuses on defects in volition or self-control. The substantial capacity test (Model Penal Code) focuses on reason and self-control. Insanity is an affirmative defense in which the actual burden of proof varies, depending on the jurisdiction.

John Hinckley, who attempted to assassinate President Reagan, was found not guilty by reason of insanity. This verdict troubled many and may have been caused by the fact that the prosecution was required to prove that Hinckley was sane beyond a reasonable doubt. Subsequent federal legislation places the burden on the defendant to prove their insanity by clear and convincing evidence. Some states have also changed their law, placing the burden of proof on the defendant. The federal government shifted the burden of proof to the defendant by clear and convincing evidence and eliminated any volitional test of insanity.

Diminished capacity involves mental disease or defect that will not qualify for the insanity defense. It may reduce the degree of a crime, because it impairs the capacity to specific intent. If successful, it may reduce the crime to a lower level or complete acquittal because the required *mens rea* cannot be proven. The insanity defense leads to a special verdict.

Age can excuse criminal liability; it can also increase it. At common law, there was an irrebuttable presumption that a child under seven couldn't form criminal intent. Between seven and fourteen, there was a refutable presumption of incapacity to form intent. At age fourteen, children were presumed to be capable of forming intent. Many states follow some updated form of the common law. All jurisdictions now have juvenile courts and special laws for juveniles. Juveniles over a certain age who commit serious crimes can be tried in criminal courts as adults.

Duress can be an excuse when individuals are threatened and forced to commit a crime or be killed. In most states, duress is not a defense to murder.

At common law, and in most, if not all, states, voluntary intoxication was not a defense. While voluntary intoxication is not an excuse, involuntary intoxication is a defense.

Entrapment occurs when law enforcement officers actively induce, trick, or persuade individuals to commit crimes they otherwise wouldn't commit. There are two main types of entrapment defenses. The subjective version focuses on whether or not the defendant was predisposed to commit the crime anyway. The objective version focuses on whether the government action would cause a reasonable, law-abiding person to commit a crime.

Various types of syndromes or conditions such as post-traumatic stress disorder and premenstrual syndrome (PMS) have been tried as defenses. In general, they are not successful.

PRACTICE TEST BANK

MULTIPLE CHOICE

1. If diminished capacity evidence is utilized in an intentional homicide case, the result of accepting the evidence is _____.

    a. not guilty of any type of homicide
    b. reducing the homicide to a lower degree homicide
    c. not guilty by reason of insanity
    d. a verdict of not guilty by reason of diminished capacity

2. The only states that adopted the _____ rule (or product test) for the insanity defense were Maine and New Hampshire.

    a. Durham
    b. M'Naghten
    c. substantial capacity
    d. right-wrong

3. To establish the duress defense in most jurisdictions, it must be shown that the threat of harm against the defendant was _____.

    a. contingent
    b. foreseeable
    c. overt
    d. reasonably believed to be real

4. In the substantial capacity test, the traditional word "know" has been replaced by the word _____.

    a. understand
    b. comprehend
    c. appreciate
    d. aggrandize

5. The objective test of entrapment focuses on government action that _____.

    a. would cause a law-abiding person to commit a crime
    b. provides an opportunity for criminally inclined individuals to commit a crime
    c. would cause a predisposed person to commit a crime
    d. provides an opportunity for a predisposed person to commit a crime

6. Which of the following is not a valid legal excuse for crime?

    a. insanity
    b. voluntary intoxication
    c. entrapment
    d. duress

7. Only the excuse of _____, when raised as a successful defense, does not result in a complete acquittal and immediate release from custody.

    a. entrapment
    b. duress
    c. involuntary intoxication
    d. insanity

8. The M'Naghten test of insanity is referred to as the _____ test.

    a. right-wrong
    b. Durham
    c. McDonough
    d. product

9. The _____ test of insanity deals only with defendant's inability to control their conduct.

    a. product
    b. right-wrong
    c. M'Naghten
    d. irresistible impulse

10. The Model Penal Code's _____ test of insanity incorporates both the cognitive and volitional components of other tests.

    a. Durham
    b. M'Naghten
    c. product
    d. substantial capacity

11. The defense of diminished capacity is available _____.

    a. in most states for most offenses
    b. in most states only when the insanity defense is raised
    c. in most states, but for felonies only
    d. only in few states

12. Most jurisdictions utilize some form of the Model Penal Code's _____ test for their insanity defense.

    a. substantial capacity
    b. Durham
    c. irresistible impulse
    d. product

13. In the 1980s, many states and the federal government changed their _____ defenses, after the verdict in the trial of John Hinckley.

    a. duress
    b. diminished capacity
    c. entrapment
    d. insanity

14. The _____ test of insanity incorporates some of the ideas of both the right-wrong and irresistible impulse test.

    a. product
    b Durham
    c. diminished capacity
    d. substantial capacity

15. The defense of diminished capacity _____.

    a. is the same as the right-wrong insanity test
    b. involves a claim that mental illness (but not quite insanity) kept the defendant from having the required intent
    c. asserts that the defendant's acts were involuntary
    d. is the same as diminished responsibility

16. At common law, there was an irrebuttable presumption that children under _____ could not form criminal intent.

    a. seven
    b. eight
    c. ten
    d. twelve

17. After the Hinckley insanity verdict, Congress changed the burden of proof for the federal insanity defense. The burden of proof is now on the defendant to prove insanity _____.

    a. by a preponderance of the evidence
    b. beyond a reasonable doubt
    c. by clear and convincing evidence
    d. beyond reasonable suspicion

18. Under the common law, when children reached the age of _____, they were presumed to be capable of criminal intent, just like adults.

    a. seven
    b. twelve
    c. fourteen
    d. seventeen

19. The subjective test of entrapment is an attempt to deal with _____.

    a. organized crime
    b. predisposed criminals
    c. government abuses
    d. young offenders

20. At common law, voluntary intoxication was a/n _____.

    a. justification
    b. defense
    c. mitigating factor
    d. aggravating factor

21. Combat soldiers and others subjected to extreme situations that later commit crimes sometimes attempt to use the _____ defense.

    a. PMS
    b. post-traumatic stress syndrome
    c. chronic fatigue syndrome
    d. traumatic automaton stress induced

22. The objective test of entrapment is so named because the test revolves around _____.

    a. subjective reactions to police conduct
    b. whether an objectively predisposed person would commit the crime
    c. how a hypothetical, reasonable person would react
    d. public attitudes toward the seriousness of the crime

23. When offenders raise age as a defense, they are claiming _____.

    a. they are too young to be tried in an adult court
    b. they are too young to have the capacity to be responsible for their behavior
    c. the prosecution must show that they are mature enough to be tried
    d. they are too old to be tried and incarcerated for their behavior

24. Which of the following tests of insanity is totally volitional?

    a. substantial capacity
    b. M'Naghten
    c. Durham
    d. irresistible impulse

25. The court does not have to consider the _____ when deciding to allow a waiver.

    a. seriousness of the offense
    b. sophistication and maturity of the juvenile
    c. precipitation by the victim
    d. threat the juvenile poses to public safety

26. Excuses tend to involve either _____ people or circumstances.

    a. mitigating
    b. codependent
    c. abnormal
    d. contingent

27. The hypothetical situation of a man who believes he's squeezing lemons but is really strangling his wife to death is an example of the _____ approach to insanity.

    a. subjective
    b. cognitive
    c. volitional
    d. objective

28. Under the Model Penal Code test of insanity, the defendant must lack _____ mental control.

    a. total
    b. complete
    c. partial
    d. substantial

29. Which of the following is an excuse, rather than a justification?

    a. duress
    b. necessity
    c. self-defense
    d. defense of others

30. In a majority of states, the defense of _____ cannot be used to a charge of murder.

    a. entrapment
    b. insanity
    c. duress
    d. involuntary intoxication

TRUE/FALSE

1. The cognition form of the insanity defense deals with the will or ability to control conduct.
    a. true
    b. false

2. Most jurisdictions utilize the subjective test of entrapment.
    a. true
    b. false

3. The irresistible impulse test is a cognitive type of insanity defense.
    a. true
    b. false

4. The Durham version of the insanity defense was first announced in a famous English case in 1843.
    a. true
    b. false

5. Most states use some version of the Model Penal Code substantial capacity test of insanity.
    a. true
    b. false

6. The substantial capacity test has both cognitive and volitional elements.
    a. true
    b. false

7. Most defendants who utilize the insanity defense at trial do so unsuccessfully.
   a. true
   b. false

8. Defendants usually succeed when they argue syndrome defenses such as PMS or post-traumatic stress disorder.
   a. true
   b. false

9. In criminal law, the insanity defense is a medical concept, not a legal one.
   a. true
   b. false

10. In all states and the federal courts, the prosecution must disprove insanity by a preponderance of the evidence.
    a. true
    b. false

11. At common law, voluntary intoxication was a defense.
    a. true
    b. false

12. Involuntary intoxication is a recognized defense in most states.
    a. true
    b. false

13. A defendant who succeeds with the diminished capacity defense will automatically be committed to a mental hospital.
    a. true
    b. false

14. At common law, a child under twelve years of age could not be guilty of a criminal offense.
    a. true
    b. false

15. In most states, the defense of duress cannot be used in murder prosecutions.
    a. true
    b. false

16. To have a successful duress defense, the defendant must retreat before using force if it can be done safely.
    a. true
    b. false

17. The predisposition of the defendant to commit the crime is relevant in the subjective test of entrapment.
    a.   false
    b.   true

18. Current federal statutes use the Durham test of insanity.
    a.   true
    b.   false

19. A defendant who has prior convictions for similar offenses would probably fare best in a jurisdiction that uses the objective test of entrapment.
    a.   true
    b.   false

20. Persons found not guilty by reason of insanity spend much less time in custody than do defendants convicted of the same offenses.
    a.   true
    b.   false

21. In an excuse, the defendant admits doing the act, but argues that the act was right or justified.
    a.   true
    b.   false

22. The John Hinckley trial and verdict stimulated considerable change in the law of insanity.
    a.   true
    b.   false

23. Under the irresistible impulse test, the defendant does not have to be suffering from a mental disease or defect.
    a.   true
    b.   false

24. The defense of insanity is limited to murder cases.
    a.   true
    b.   false

25. Since the late 1980s, most jurisdictions and the federal government have abolished the insanity defense.
    a.   true
    b.   false

FILL-IN-THE-BLANK

1. The defense of _____ is recognized in only a few states.

2. _____ intoxication is not a defense.

3. The M'Naghten test of insanity is also known as the _____ test.

4. At common law, a child under the age of _____ could not be guilty of a crime.

5. The diminished capacity defense relates to negating the _____ element of crimes.

6. The Durham or_____ test of insanity basically asks if the mental illness caused the crime.

7. Under the _____ test of entrapment, the government cannot introduce evidence of the defendant's prior convictions for similar offenses.

8. If government agents offer inducements to get persons to commit crimes, this could implicate the _____ defense.

9. To establish the insanity defense, it must be shown that the defendant suffered from a mental disease or _____.

10. In some states, a defendant who is not insane but is mentally ill may be able to use the defense of _____.

11. The _____ test of entrapment focuses on the predisposition of the defendant to commit the crime.

12. In federal courts, and in many states, the burden of proof on the insanity defense is on the _____.

13. At one time, the state of _____ had the diminished capacity defense but later abolished it because of public hostility.

14. At common law, a child was presumed capable of criminal intent upon reaching the age of _____.

15. Young offenders are typically dealt with in _____ court rather than adult criminal court.

ESSAY

1. Discuss the common law rules on age and criminality and compare it with the current approach.

2. Discuss the criticisms to each of the four major tests of insanity.

3. Compare and contrast the insanity and diminished capacity defenses.

4. Compare and contrast the two major approaches to the entrapment defense.

5. Compare and contrast involuntary and voluntary intoxication as defenses to crime.

CHAPTER 6 ANSWER KEY

Multiple Choice

1. b	2. a	3. d	4. c	5. d
6. b	7. d	8. a	9. d	10. d
11. d	12. a	13. d	14. d	15. b
16. a	17. c	18. c	19. b	20. d
21. b	22. c	23. b	24. d	25. c
26. c	27. b	28. d	29. a	30. c

True/False

1. F	2. T	3. F	4. F	5. T
6. T	7. T	8. F	9. F	10. F
11. F	12. T	13. F	14. F	15. T
16. F	17. T	18. F	19. T	20. F
21. F	22. T	23. F	24. F	25. F

Fill-in-the-Blank

1. diminished capacity
2. Voluntary
3. right-wrong
4. seven
5. *mens rea*
6. product
7. objective
8. entrapment
9. defect
10. diminished capacity
11. subjective
12. defendant
13. California
14. fourteen
15. juvenile

CHAPTER 7
PARTIES TO CRIME AND VICARIOUS LIABILITY

LEARNING OBJECTIVES

After studying this chapter, students will understand that:

- Participants before and during the commission of crimes are guilty of the crime itself.

- Participants after the commission of crimes are guilty of a separate, less serious offense.

- The core idea of accessory liability is that it's not as blameworthy to help someone else escape prosecution and punishment as it is to participate in the crime itself.

- Vicarious liability has to be created by statute.

- Vicarious liability can apply either to enterprise (mainly business) or to individuals.

KEY TERMS AND CONCEPTS

complicity—the principle regarding parties to crime that establishes the conditions under which more than one person incurs liability before, during, and after committing crimes; when one person is liable for another person's crime; p. 208

vicarious liability—the principle of liability for another based on relationship; p. 208

accomplices—the parties liable as principals before and during a crime; p. 209

accessories—the parties liable for separate, lesser offenses following a crime; p. 209

Pinkerton rule—the rule that conspiracy and the underlying crime are separate offenses; p. 209

mere presence rule—a person's presence at the scene of a crime doesn't by itself satisfy the *actus reus* requirement of accomplice liability; p. 210

CHAPTER OUTLINE

I. There are two types of liability for someone else's criminal act:
    A. Complicity—Parties-to-crime laws establish when a person can be held liable for the crimes of another.
    B. Vicarious liability laws establish which types of relationships can create criminal liability.

II. Parties to Crime
    A. There were four types of parties to crime at common law:
        1. Principals in the first degree actually commit the crime.
        2. Principles in the second degree are present when the crimes are committed.
        3. Accessories-before-the-fact
            a. Help before the crime is committed
            b. Are not present when the crime is committed
        4. Accessories-after-the-fact help after the crime is committed.

III. Participation before and during the commission of a crime—Accomplices are prosecuted for committing the crime itself (helping a murderer is murder).
    A. **Accomplice *actus reus***
        1. Core idea—accomplice took some positive act to help commit a crime.
        2. Words can be accomplice *actus reus*.
        3. Presence at the crime scene isn't enough unless there's a duty (parent to minor child).
        4. Actions after the crime can be relevant to prove *actus reus*.
        5. *Case: State v. Ulvinen*
    B. **Accomplice *mens rea***
        1. Purpose clearly qualifies.
        2. Jurisdictions vary and sometimes are confused as to whether knowledge, recklessness, or negligence qualify.
        3. *Case: U.S. v. Peoni*
        4. *Case: People v. Poplar*
        5. *Case: Lewis et. al. v. State*
        6. *Case: State v. Foster*

IV. Participation after the commission of a crime—Accessory
        1. A separate, lesser offense than accomplice liability
        2. Elements of accessory after the fact
            a. Accessory personally helped the person who committed the felony (*actus reus* element).
            b. Accessory knew a felony was committed (*mens rea* element).
            c. Accessory helped for the purpose of hindering prosecution (*mens rea* element).
            d. Someone other than the accessory actually committed a felony (circumstance element).

3. *Case: State v. Chism*
4. *Dunn v. Commonwealth*

V. Vicarious Liability.
　A. Vicarious liability makes one liable for the acts of another because of a relationship.

VI. Enterprise Vicarious Liability
　A. Pinpointing responsibility is difficult because of the complexity of organizations and the number of people making decisions.
　B. Distinguishing vicarious liability from strict liability: strict liability eliminates the *mens rea* requirement; vicarious liability transfers the *actus reus* and *mens rea* of an employee to the corporation.
　C. Constitutional and policy issues
　　　1. Due process issues
　　　　　a. Liability is based on relationship and not acts and/or intent.
　　　　　b. Fairness to shareholders, who usually pay the fines
　　　2. Policy question—deterrence?
　D. *Case: State v. Zeta Chi Fraternity*

VII. Individual Vicarious Liability—can be established by statute, not by courts (meaning there is no common-law vicarious liability)
　A. *Case: State v. Tomaino*
　B. Traffic violations—difficulty proving who parked the vehicle
　　　2. *Prima facie* case—presumes driver was the operator and is responsible
　C. Parental responsibility—parents responsible for acts of children
　　　1. *Case: State v. Akers*
　　　2. Distinguish traditional parental liability statutes which hold parents liable for failure to supervise their child (omission is the parents *actus reus*) with vicarious liability statutes which hold parents responsible for the acts committed by their child.

CHAPTER SUMMARY

A person can be criminally liable for the criminal acts of another. The doctrine of complicity (parties to crime) establishes when you can be held criminally liable for someone else's crimes. The doctrine of vicarious liability establishes what types of relationships can make you liable for someone else's crimes.

The common law on complicity was complex. A principal in the first degree was the person who actually committed the crime. Principals in the second degree were those who were present at the scene of the crime and aided the principal in the first degree. Such aid could take the form of being a lookout or driving the getaway car. Accessories-before-the-fact were those who were involved in the crime before it was committed and were not present when it was committed. An example would be a person who provides safe-cracking tools for the safecracker. Finally, an accessory-after-the-fact is one whose only aid comes after the crime was completed.

Today, the law has been simplified. Under the current approach, participants before and during the commission of crimes are guilty of the crime itself. These persons are liable as accomplices. Participants after the commission of crimes are guilty of a separate, less serious offense.

Liability as an accomplice is different than liability as a co-conspirator. Persons in a conspiracy to commit a crime can also be liable for both the conspiracy and the crimes of other conspirators. This flows from the Pinkerton rule. The crime in conspiracy is the agreement to commit the other crime.

The essence of accomplice *actus reus* is that the accomplice took some positive action to aid or assist in the commission of a crime actually committed by another. The *mens rea* of complicity varies, depending on the jurisdiction. It may be purpose, knowledge, recklessness, or negligence. The core idea of accessory liability is that it's not as blameworthy to help someone else escape prosecution as it is to participate in the crime itself.

Mens rea in business crimes is hard to prove because of the size and complexity of organizations and decision-making. Legislatures attempt to overcome this by creating strict liability crimes (eliminating any *mens rea*) and/or creating vicarious liability. Vicarious liability raises due process constitutional issues and policy questions about its effectiveness.

Individual vicarious liability involves making an individual responsible for the acts of other individuals: for instance, making owners of cars vicariously liable for operators' parking tickets. The liability is created because of the owner-operator relationship.

Vicarious liability of parents based on the parent-child relationship grew out of public fear, frustration, and anger over juvenile crime. There is little case law on such statutes, and some have been held unconstitutional.

PRACTICE TEST BANK

MULTIPLE CHOICE

1. The _____ rule or principle states that everyone who is involved in a crime, whether before, during, or after, may be responsible for that crime.

    a. vicarious liability
    b. complicity
    c. Pinkerton
    d. Wharton

2. Mr. A robs the bank. Mr. B waits outside with the getaway car. Under the common law, with regard to the bank robbery, Mr. B is a/n _____.

    a. principal in the first degree
    b. accessory-after-the-fact
    c. accessory-before-the-fact
    d. principal in the second degree

3. Mr. A commits a burglary. A few days before, he got the burglary tools from Mr. B., who has no other involvement in the burglary. Under the common law approach, Mr. B is a/n _____.

    a. accessory-before-the-fact
    b. accessory-after-the-fact
    c. principle in the third degree
    d. principal in the second degree

4. An agreement between two or more persons to commit a crime is a/n _____.

    a. solicitation
    b. conspiracy
    c. complicity crime
    d. vicarious liability offense

5. The current approach to complicity _____.

    a. maintains most of the common law distinctions
    b. eliminates the principle and accessory classifications of the common law
    c. retains the common law terminology of accessories before the fact
    d. retains the common law terminology of principal in the second degree

6. Accomplice liability _____.

   a. requires *actus reus* but not *mens rea*
   b. requires *mens rea* but no *actus reus*
   c. requires both *actus reus* and *mens rea*
   d. is a strict liability offense

7. The Pinkerton rule is applicable only to _____.

   a. accomplices
   b. the doctrine of complicity
   c. conspiracies
   d. accessories

8. Vicarious liability arises most frequently in employment or _____ relationships.

   a. personal
   b. producer-consumer
   c. family
   d. business

9. To convict a person of being an accessory-after-the-fact, the government must show that _____.

   a. the person intended to aid the criminal after the crime
   b. there was a conspiracy to aid after the crime that was entered into before the crime
   c. the Pinkerton rule applies
   d. the person provided aid to a person whom he knew had committed a misdemeanor

10. In general, merely being present at the scene of a crime _____.

    a. is sufficient to create accomplice liable
    b. is not sufficient to create accomplice liability
    c. is the *actus reus* of accomplice liability
    d. creates a presumption that there was a conspiracy to commit the crime

11. To assist in proving corporate liability, legislatures and prosecutor typically rely on two doctrines, _____.

    a. conspiracy and complicity
    b. strict and complicity liability
    c. principal and accessory liability
    d. strict and vicarious liability

12. In *State v. Akers*, the New Hampshire appellate court overturned the parents' vicarious liability conviction for acts of their children because the law _____.

    a. violated equal protection because it applied only to parents
    b. violated substantive due process by punishing parenthood
    c. was a bill of attainder
    d. was overbroad

13. Mere presence of the actor at the scene of a crime may create accomplice liability if _____.

    a. the actor has a duty to prevent the crime and fails to prevent or attempt to prevent it
    b. the actor secretly hopes the crime will be completed
    c. the actor knows the victim but does not intervene
    d. the actor knows the criminal but does not intervene

14. The case of *State v. Walden*, in which the defendant was charged for not preventing her one-year-old son from being beaten, illustrates _____.

    a. the exception to the mere presence rule
    b. the exception to the rule against accessories-after-the-fact
    c. the rule of vicarious liability
    d. the rule of accomplice liability

15. The rule that the conspiracy to commit a crime and the crimes committed pursuant to the conspiracy are separate offenses is called the _____ rule.

    a. Wharton
    b. Peoni
    c. Brady
    d. Pinkerton

16. The _____ of accomplice liability is frequently phrased in terms of aiding, abetting, or assisting another who commits a crime.

    a. *mens rea*
    b. *actus reus*
    c. circumstances
    d. concurrence

17. According to the U.S. Supreme Court in *Bailey v. U.S.* (1969), flight from the scene of a crime _____.

    a. by itself proves accomplice liability
    b. by itself proves guilty of the crime
    c. is not evidence of accomplice liability
    d. by itself cannot prove accomplice liability

18. In *State v. Ulvinen* (1983), the Minnesota appellate court held that _____ alone could not prove accomplice liability for murder.

    a. being related to the victim
    b. living in the same household as the victim
    c. passive approval of the crime
    d. refusing to cooperate with the police

19. The rule of the Peoni case requires that the accomplice not only intended to aid the offender and knew of the crime to be committed, but that the accomplice also intended or desired that _____.

    a. the crime be committed
    b. there be a conspiracy
    c. the actual offender not be caught
    d. the accomplice not be caught

20. The early decisions on accomplice liability held that the only *mens rea* required for accomplice liability was intent _____.

    a. to aid the offender knowing a crime would be committed
    b. to form a conspiracy
    c. that the offender commit the crime
    d. to benefit from the crime committed

21. Crimes involving being an accessory-after-the-fact typically have _____ *mens rea* element(s).

    a. one
    b. two
    c. three
    d. four

22. Most accessory-after-the-fact criminal statutes contain _____ circumstance element(s).

    a. no
    b. one
    c. two
    d. three

23. Unlike accomplice liability, vicarious liability does not require that the person being held vicariously liable _____.

    a. participate in the crime
    b. be aware of the circumstances
    c. be involved in a conspiracy
    d. not be involved in a conspiracy

24. Strict liability crimes have no _____.

    a. *actus reus* element
    b. voluntary act element
    c. legality requirement
    d. *mens rea* element

25. Vicarious liability is based on _____.

    a. benefiting from the crime
    b. being involved in the crime
    c. relationships
    d. personal *actus reus* and *mens rea*

26. Vicarious liability of individuals usually involves _____.

    a. homicides
    b. traffic tickets
    c. felonies
    d. conspiracies

27. _____ laws make parents liable for the crimes of their children, if the parents fail to supervise and control their children.

    a. Parental responsibility
    b. Vicarious parental liability
    c. Conspiracy
    d. Parental combination

Study Guide

28. Corporate liability is always a form of _____ liability.

   a. co-conspirator
   b. accomplice
   c. accessory
   d. vicarious

29. If the owner of a vehicle is *prima facie* responsible for parking tickets issued on that vehicle, this means that the owner _____.

   a. is guilty of conspiracy regarding the violation
   b. is presumed responsible for the violation
   c. is an accomplice to the violation
   d. is an accessory to the violation

30. Many vicarious liability statutes _____.

   a. violate due process, the presumption of innocence, and the Eighth Amendment
   c. are felony statutes
   d. are also strict liability statutes
   e. require that the prosecution prove a conspiracy

TRUE/FALSE

1. Complicity creates liability because of a relationship with the offender.
   a. true
   b. false

2. Vicarious liability hinges on providing aid or assistance to an offender.
   a. true
   b. false

3. At common law, the person who actually committed the crime is the principal in the first degree.
   a. true
   b. false

4. A co-conspirator could be an accessory-before-the-fact.
   a. true
   b. false

5. The Pinkerton rule states that accomplices are liable for all crimes committed by the persons they aid.
   a. true
   b. false

112

6. The doctrine of complicity establishes when one person can be criminally liable for the acts of another.
   a. true
   b. false

7. At common law, a person who knowingly harbored a felony fugitive to prevent the felon's capture would be an accessory-after-the-fact.
   a. true
   b. false

8. At common law, a person who acted as a lookout for another criminal would be a principal in the third degree.
   a. true
   b. false

9. A person who aids, abets, or assists another in committing a crime is an accomplice to that crime.
   a. true
   b. false

10. Flight from the scene of a crime is enough evidence to convict of a crime or being an accomplice.
    a. true
    b. false

11. Mere presence at the scene of a crime is, all by itself, not enough to convict one of being an accomplice to that crime.
    a. true
    b. false

12. Barring some duty to the victim, passive approval of a crime is, by itself, enough to warrant conviction as an accomplice.
    a. true
    b. false

13. Early court decisions on accomplice liability did not require proof of intent to facilitate the crime, only proof of intent to aid the criminal.
    a. true
    b. false

14. The minority rule is that in addition to general intent, accomplice liability also requires intent that the crime be committed.
    a. true
    b. false

15. A person cannot be held liable as an accomplice for negligent or reckless acts.
    a. true
    b. false

16. Most accessory-after-the-fact statutes require that the defendant know the person they aided committed a felony.
    a. true
    b. false

17. Accessory and accomplice liability can be established by circumstantial evidence.
    a. true
    b. false

18. A strict liability offense has no *actus reus* element.
    a. true
    b. false

19. Corporations cannot be vicariously liable for the acts of their employees.
    a. true
    b. false

20. Many offenses related to businesses and corporations are both strict and vicarious liability.
    a. true
    b. false

21. A person can be vicariously liable even though they personally did no act and had no criminal intent.
    a. true
    b. false

22. A person who is *prima facie* responsible is presumed responsible.
    a. true
    b. false

23. Parental responsibility laws make parents liable if their children commit a crime because the parents failed to supervise or control their children.
    a. true
    b. false

24. Every law imposing vicarious criminal liability on parents for the acts of their children has been found to be constitutional.
    a. true
    b. false

25. Statutes that impose both strict and vicarious liability always violate due process.
    a. true
    b. false

FILL-IN-THE-BLANK

1. Laws making parents liable for acts of offspring because of failure to control or supervise are called _____ laws.

2. At common law, persons who protected or harbored the felon after the felony was completed were called accessories-after-the-_____.

3. The doctrine of _____ sometimes makes persons liable for the acts of others.

4. _____ makes one liable for the acts of another because of the relationship to the other.

5. At common law, the person who actually committed the crime was termed a _____ in the first degree.

6. At common law, persons who assisted the criminal before the crime was committed were called _____.

7. At common law, persons involved in a crime who were present at the scene of the crime were termed _____.

8. In most jurisdictions today, participants before and/or during the crime are called _____.

9. An agreement to commit a crime is called a/n _____.

10. Under the _____ rule, conspirators can be convicted of both conspiracy and the crime committed.

11. The term _____ means adequate to establish a presumption of guilt.

12. A crime without a *mens rea* element is called a/n _____ crime.

13. A well-established rule states that _____ at the scene of a crime is, alone, not enough to justify conviction as an accomplice.

14. Aiding, abetting, assisting, etc. are the *actus reus* of _____.

15. In many modern codes, a person who assists a criminal after the crime is called a/n _____.

Study Guide

ESSAY

1. Discuss the four parties to a crime under the common law. Provide an example of each.

2. Discuss the differences between accomplice liability under modern statutes and the common law. What advantages or disadvantages are their under each approach? Give examples.

3. Describe, define, compare, and contrast accomplice and vicarious liability. Be sure to provide examples.

4. Why does the government find it necessary to use vicarious liability and strict liability crimes to fight corporate crime? Be sure to provide examples.

5. What are the four elements of most accessory-after-the-fact statutes? Provide an example of each element.

CHAPTER 7 ANSWER KEY

Multiple Choice

1. b	2. d	3. a	4. b	5. b
6. c	7. c	8. d	9. a	10. b
11. d	12. b	13. a	14. a	15. d
16. b	17. d	18. c	19. a	20. a
21. b	22. b	23. a	24. d	25. c
26. b	27. a	28. d	29. b	30. d

True/False

1. F	2. F	3. T	4. T	5. F
6. T	7. T	8. F	9. T	10. F
11. T	12. F	13. T	14. T	15. F
16. T	17. T	18. F	19. F	20. T
21. T	22. T	23. T	24. F	25. F

Fill-in-the-Blank

1. parental responsibility
2. fact
3. complicity
4. Vicarious liability
5. principal
6. accessories-before-the-fact
7. principals in the second degree
8. accomplices
9. conspiracy
10. Pinkerton
11. *prima facie*
12. strict liability
13. mere presence
14. accomplice liability
15. accessory

CHAPTER 8
INCHOATE CRIMES:
ATTEMPT, CONSPIRACY AND SOLICITATION

LEARNING OBJECTIVES

After studying this chapter, students will understand that:

- Inchoate offenses punish people for crimes they haven't finished committing.

- Inchoate offenses require some action but not enough to complete the crime intended.

- Liability for criminal attempt offenses is based on two rationales: preventing dangerous conduct and neutralizing dangerous people.

- The *mens rea* of inchoate crimes is *always* the purpose or specific intent to commit a specific crime.

- The *actus reus* of attempt is an action that's beyond mere preparation but not enough to complete the crime.

- Legal impossibility is a defense to attempt liability; factual impossibility isn't.

- Voluntary and complete abandonment of an attempt in progress is a defense to attempt liability in some states.

- Punishing conspiracy and solicitation to commit a crime is based on nipping in the bud the special danger of group criminality.

KEY TERMS AND CONCEPTS

- **criminal attempt**—intending to commit a crime and taking steps to complete it but something interrupts the completion of the crime's commission; p. 234

- **criminal conspiracy**—agreement between two or more persons to commit a crime; p. 234

- **criminal solicitation**—urging another person to commit a crime, even though the person doesn't respond to the urging; p. 234

- **inchoate offenses**—offenses based on crimes not yet completed; p. 234

Chapter 8: Inchoate Crimes—Attempt, Conspiracy, and Solicitation

- **offenses of general application**—describes the inchoate crimes, which are partly general and partly specific; p. 234

- **dangerous act rationale (in attempt law)**—looking at how closely a defendant came to completing a crime; p. 236

- **dangerous person rationale (attempt law)**—looking at how fully a defendant developed a criminal purpose to commit a crime; p. 236

- **attempt *mens rea***—specific intent to commit a crime that's never completed; p. 237

- **attempt *actus reus***—steps taken to complete a crime that's never actually completed; p. 240

- **last proximate act rule**—your acts brought you as close as possible to completing the crime; p. 240

- **proximity tests**—tests of dangerous conduct: physical proximity, dangerous proximity, and indispensable element; p. 241

- **dangerous proximity test to success test/physical proximity test**—looking at the seriousness of the offense intended; the closeness to completion of the crime; and the probability the conduct would actually have resulted in completion of the crime; p. 241

- **indispensable element test (attempt law)**—asks whether defendants have gotten control of everything they need to complete the crime; p. 242

- **unequivocality test/*res ipsa loquiter* test ("act speaks for itself")**—examines the likelihood the defendant won't complete the crime (attempt law); p. 242

- **probable desistance test**—a dangerous person test that focuses on how far defendants have gone, not on what's left for them to do to complete the crime; p. 242-43

- **"substantial steps" test (in attempt *actus reus*)**—in the Model Penal Code, substantial acts toward completion of a crime that strongly corroborate the actor's intent to commit the crime; p. 243

- **legal impossibility**—the defense that what the actor attempted was not a "crime;" p. 248

- **factual impossibility**—the defense that some extraneous factor made it impossible to complete a crime; p. 248

- **extraneous factor**—a condition beyond the attempter's control; p. 248

- **defense of voluntary abandonment**—the actor voluntarily and completely gives up his criminal purpose before completing the offense; p. 253

- **conspiracy**—agreeing to commit a crime; p. 256

- **conspiracy *actus reus***—consists of two parts: 1) an agreement to commit a crime (in all states) and 2) an overt act in furtherance of the agreement (in about half the states); p. 257

- **conspiracy *mens rea***—specific intent to commit a crime, or specific intent to commit a legal act by illegal means; p. 260

- **overt act (in conspiracy)**—requirement of conspiracy *actus reus* of some act toward completing the crime in addition to the agreement; p. 258

- **criminal objective**—the criminal goal of an agreement to commit a crime; p. 261

- **unilateral approach**—(in conspiracy) not all the conspirators need to agree to commit a crime to impose criminal liability (conspiracy *actus reus*); p. 261

- **wheel conspiracies**—one or more defendants participate in every transaction; p. 261

- **chain conspiracies**—participants at one end of the chain may know nothing of those at the other end, but every participant handles the same commodity at different points, such as manufacture, distribution, and sale; p. 262

- **solicitation**—trying to get someone to commit a crime; p. 263

- **solicitation *actus reus***—urging another person to commit a crime; p. 264

- **solicitation *mens rea***—intent to get another person to commit a crime; p. 264

CHAPTER OUTLINE

I. Inchoate crimes are incomplete crimes.
    A. Inchoate comes from the Latin "to begin."
    B. Inchoate crimes are separate crimes of starting but not finishing any other crime.
    C. Whether to make it a crime to start but not finish committing the crime poses a problem:
        1. Is the law punishing someone who has done no harm or setting someone free who is determined to do harm?
        2. Dilemma of criminal attempt law is resolved through three requirements:
            a. Requiring specific intent
            b. Requiring some action
            c. Punishing inchoate crimes less severely than completed crimes

D. Three types of inchoate offenses:
   1. Attempt—trying to commit a crime
   2. Conspiracy—agreeing to commit a crime
   3. Solicitation—trying to get someone else to commit a crime
E. All inchoate offenses are specific intent crimes.

II. **Attempt**—An attempt is a failed effort to complete a crime.
   A. **Attempt History**
      1. Began with "excessive leniency"
      2. In the 1500s and 1600s, modern attempt law began punishing attempts more seriously.
      3. By the 1800s, attempts to commit indictable offenses were misdemeanors.
   B. **Rationales** for criminal attempt law
      1. Dangerous act rationale—prevent harm from dangerous conduct (focuses on how close to completion the crime is)
      2. Dangerous person rationale—neutralize dangerous people (focuses on how developed the criminal purpose is)
      3. Both (1) and (2) look at actions taken to measure the danger.
   C. **Elements** of Attempt
      1. **Attempt m*ens rea***
         a. Purpose or specific intent always present
         b. No knowing, reckless, or negligent attempts
      2. **Attempt a*ctus reus***
         a. How much action is enough?
            (1) Preparation isn't enough to qualify as the *actus reus* of attempt.
            (2) Toughest problem in criminal attempt is drawing a line between preparation and attempt.
         b. Tests to help draw the line between preparation and the act of attempt:
            (1) Physical proximity test
               (a) Focus on
                  (i) Dangerous conduct, not dangerous people
                  (ii) What's left to do, not what's already done
               (b) Completion of all but the last act needed to accomplish the crime is surely enough, but so are acts falling short of this point, including:
                  (i) Indispensable element test—defendants who've gotten control of everything they need to complete the crime
                  (ii) Dangerous proximity test—defendants have gotten dangerously close to completing the crime
            (2) Unequivocality (probable desistance) test
               (a) Focus on
                  (i) Dangerous persons, not dangerous conduct
                  (ii) What's already done, not what's left to do
               (b) Unequivocality test asks whether an ordinary person observing defendants' actions without knowing their intent would guess they were determined to commit the crime.

                (3) "Substantial steps" (Model Penal Code) test
                    (a) Purpose—clarify and simplify other tests
                    (b) Focus on
                        (i) Dangerous persons
                        (ii) What's already done, not what's left to do
                    (c) Definition—substantial steps that "strongly corroborate" defendant's criminal purpose
    D. **Impossibility** of completing the crime as a defense
        1. Legal impossibility is a defense to criminal attempt; factual impossibility is not.
        2. Legal impossibility
            a. Defendants intend to commit crimes, do everything they can to complete the crime, but what they intend and do isn't a crime.
            b. Is a defense
        3. Factual impossibility
            a. Defendants intend to commit a crime and take all the steps necessary to complete it, but a fact makes it impossible to complete.
            b. People bent on committing crimes shouldn't benefit from a stroke of luck—this isn't a defense.
    E. **Abandonment** of attempts as a defense
        1. Complete and voluntary abandonment of attempt is an affirmative defense in about half the states.
        2. Arguments in favor of the abandonment defense
            a. People who voluntarily and completely give up their criminal attempts aren't dangerous.
            b. We want to encourage people who are just about to hurt someone or their property to give up their plans.
        3. Argument against defense of abandonment—It encourages bad people to take the early steps in committing crimes because they know they won't be punished.

III. **Conspiracy** is an agreement to commit a crime.
    A. Agreeing to commit crimes (criminal conspiracy) is further removed from completed crimes than trying to commit them (criminal attempt).
    B. Justifications for conspiracy law
        1. Works hand in hand with attempt to nip criminal purpose in the bud
        2. Strikes at the special danger of group criminal activity
    C. **Conspiracy *actus reus***
        1. **Agreement** to commit a crime is the heart of the crime of conspiracy.
            a. Doesn't have to be in writing
            b. An unspoken understanding, inferred from facts and circumstances, is good enough to prove agreement.
        2. About half the states require an **"overt act"** in addition to the act of agreement.
            a. Purpose—verify the firmness of the agreement
            b. Act doesn't have to amount to much; it can be of "very small significance."

D. **Conspiracy** *mens rea*
   1. Crime of purpose (specific intent)
   2. Can mean intent to make the agreement or intent to achieve the criminal objective.
E. **Parties to conspiracy**
   1. Traditional approach—two or more individuals agreeing to commit crimes
   2. Unilateral approach—not all the conspirators had to agree to commit a crime as long as the defendant believes they did
F. **Large-scale conspiracies**
   1. Wheel conspiracies: two sets of conspirators:
      a. Hub—conspirators who participate in all transactions
      b. Spokes—conspirators who only participate in one transaction
   2. Chain conspiracies—participants at one end of the chain don't know anything of participants at the other end, but they all handle the same illegal commodity at different points (manufacture, distribution, sale).
G. **Criminal objective** of conspiracy
   1. Traditionally included everything from treason to disturbing the peace
   2. Some effort to limit the reach of conspiracy
      a. Requires an overt act in addition to an act of agreement
      b. Applies to criminal objectives only

IV. **Solicitation** is asking or encouraging someone else to commit a crime.
   A. Definition—the crime of trying to get someone else to commit a crime
   B. Arguments against criminal solicitation law
      1. The act of soliciting isn't dangerous enough to punish because an independent moral force (the person solicited) stands between the solicitation and its objective.
      2. Solicitors aren't dangerous enough people, and they prove it by needing someone else to do their dirty work.
   C. Arguments for criminal solicitation law
      1. Solicitation is another form of the danger of group criminality.
      2. Solicitors are smart masters at manipulating others to do their dirty work.
   D. **Solicitation** *actus reus* requires words that actually try to get someone to commit a crime (not just approve the commission of the crime).
   E. **Solicitation** *mens rea* requires purpose or specific intent to get someone to commit a specific crime.
   F. The **criminal objective of solicitation** varies from limiting it to violent felonies in some jurisdictions to including all crimes in other jurisdictions.

CHAPTER SUMMARY

Inchoate offenses involve punishing people for crimes they haven't completed. The term "inchoate" comes from the Latin meaning "to begin." Inchoate offenses require some action but not enough to finish the crime intended. Such offenses enable the police, courts, and corrections to intervene before the intended harm occurs. All of these offenses have both a general intent and a specific intent element. General intent is to do the act, say the words, make an agreement, etc.

Specific intent is any intent other than general intent. In these crimes, the specific intent is to commit a crime above and beyond the inchoate offense. Inchoate crimes are generally punished separately and less severely than the completed offense.

Criminal liability for criminal attempt offenses is based on two rationales—first, preventing dangerous conduct, and second, neutralizing dangerous people. The *mens rea* of inchoate crimes is the specific intent to commit a complete crime.

The *actus reus* of attempt is an action that is beyond mere preparation but not actually completion of the crime. How much action is required to make one guilty of an attempt is hotly debated, and there are a number of approaches. A proximity approach focuses on how close the defendant gets to completing the crime. An unequivocality approach focuses on whether the defendant got far enough along that stopping is unlikely. The Model Penal Code test requires that the defendant have taken substantial steps and that such steps strongly corroborate the actor's criminal intent.

Legal impossibility is a defense to attempt liability. If the defendant did everything he or she wanted to do and it still wouldn't be a crime, then it is a valid defense. The principle of legality would seem to require this. Factual impossibility is not a defense. If certain factors unknown to the defendant would make it impossible to complete the crime, this is not a defense. In some jurisdictions voluntary and complete abandonment of an attempt in progress may be a defense to attempt liability.

Solicitation and conspiracy both involve more than one person. Punishing conspiracy and solicitation to commit a crime is based not only on preventing crime but also on the special danger of group criminality.

Criminal conspiracy is the crime of agreeing with one or more people to commit a crime. The *actus reus* of conspiracy is the agreement. Some jurisdictions also require that one of the co-conspirators commit some overt act in pursuance of the conspiracy. Conspiracy is a specific intent crime. In addition to intending to agree (general intent), they must also intend to commit the planned crime.

The traditional approach to conspiracy required that at least two people really and sincerely agree to commit a crime (bilateral approach). Under this approach, a person could not be guilty of conspiring with an undercover police officer that had no intent to agree or carry out a crime. Under the unilateral approach, there can be a conspiracy even though another party does not truly agree and doesn't even know some of the others involved.

Criminal solicitation is the crime of trying to get one or more persons to commit a crime. The *actus reus* is a solicitation, command, or encouragement to commit a crime. In addition to a general intent to ask or command, there must be a specific intent that the solicited crime be completed.

Chapter 8: Inchoate Crimes—Attempt, Conspiracy, and Solicitation

PRACTICE TEST BANK

MULTIPLE CHOICE

1. The term inchoate comes from the Latin verb which means "to _____."

    a. contemplate
    b. envision
    c. begin
    d. conspire

2. All inchoate crimes are _____ crimes.

    a. specific and general intent
    b. circumstances
    c. capital
    d. redemptive

3. As compared to the completed crime, inchoate crimes are _____.

    a. always misdemeanors
    b. punished the same as the completed crime
    c. more severely punished than the completed crime
    d. less severely punished than the completed crime

4. The rationales for attempt focus on two different types of danger—_____.

    a. group activity and inciting others
    b. dangerous persons and dangerous conduct
    c. imitation and stimulation of crime
    d. group activity and stimulation of crime

5. The indispensable element test of attempt *actus reus* focuses on whether the actor _____.

    a. is likely to give up the attempt
    b. had gotten control of everything necessary to complete the crime
    c. satisfies the *res ipsa loquitur* criterion
    d. is just one step away from completing the crime

6. The Latin term *res ipsa loquitur* means the _____.

    a. thing is inherently evil
    b. thought is the origin of the act
    c. act speaks for itself
    d. intent without action is no crime

Study Guide

7. The Model Penal Code test of attempt *actus reus* requires that the defendant take _____ toward completing the crime.

   a. irreversible action
   b. substantial steps
   c. the last proximate act
   d. the next-to-last proximate act

8. The second part of the Model Penal Code test of attempt *actus reus* also requires that the defendant's actions _____.

   a. go beyond any reasonable stopping point
   b. indicate that desistance is unlikely
   c. indicate that they are dangerously close to completing the offense
   d. strongly corroborate intent to commit the crime

9. In most states, and under the Model Penal Code, which of the following would not be an attempt?

   a. lying in wait for the victim to walk by
   b. reconnoitering the planned crime scene
   c. enticing the victim to the place where the crime is planned to occur
   d. beginning to gather the materials necessary for the crime

10. The defense of ____ impossibility involves actors doing everything they can to carry out the criminal intent, but the law doesn't criminalize what they did.

    a. factual
    b. virtual
    c. legal
    d. juristic

11. The defense of ____ impossibility involves the situation where some extraneous factor interrupts or prevents completion of the crime.

    a. factual
    b. virtual
    c. real
    d. legal

12. Which of the following is a recognized form of the impossibility defense to attempt?

    a. legal
    b. factual
    c. real
    d. virtual

13. According to the appellate court in *State v. Damms*, a defendant can be guilty of the crime of attempted murder because/even though the defendant admitted to police that he _____.

    a. believed the gun was loaded (even though it was in fact unloaded)
    b. believed his wife was already dead (even though she wasn't)
    c. believed the wounds would not be fatal (even though they were)
    d. believed the police would stop him before he pointed the gun at this wife

14. Which of the following would be a valid impossibility defense?

    a. The intended victim escapes before the defendant attacks the victim.
    b. The defendant is apprehended by the police before finishing the crime.
    c. The poison is not strong enough to kill the victim.
    d. What the defendant wants to do to the victim is not a crime.

15. To be a defense to attempt, the abandonment of the attempt must be _____.

    a. caused by an extraneous factor
    b. compelled
    c. voluntary
    d. caused by police intervention

16. About half the states have a second *actus reus* element for conspiracy. They require that _____.

    a. the conspirators take a substantial step toward the crime
    b. the conspirators move beyond mere preparation
    c. one of the conspirators attempt the crime
    d. one of the conspirators do an overt act pursuant to the conspiracy

17. Mr. X conspires with Mr. Y to commit a murder. Unbeknownst to Mr. X, Mr. Y is an undercover police officer that is only trying to build a case against Mr. X. Under the unilateral approach to conspiracy, _____.

    a. both Mr. X and Mr. Y are guilty of conspiracy
    b. Mr. X is not guilty of conspiracy because there is no real agreement
    c. Mr. X has an affirmative defense
    d. Mr. X is guilty of conspiracy

18. Chain conspiracies usually involve a _____.

   a. distributor who sells to numerous dealers
   b. smuggler who has a number of wholesale customers
   c. dealer who has multiple customers
   d. pipeline from a smuggler to a distributor to a wholesaler

19. Most modern conspiracy statutes _____.

   a. limit the objective to committing a crime
   b. include any objective which is contrary to public policy
   c. limit the objective to using unlawful means to do a lawful thing
   d. include any objective which is injurious to public health

20. The federal _____ Act is a specialized conspiracy law frequently utilized against organized crime.

   a. PACO
   b. RICO
   c. CHACO
   d. OCCA

21. Which of the following is not a typical element of solicitation statutes?

   a. general intent
   b. specific intent
   c. communicating some inducement
   d. communication must be to a particular person

22. A few states restrict the crime of solicitation to solicitation of _____.

   a. felonies
   b. misdemeanors
   c. capital felonies
   d. crimes which are *mala prohibita*

23. Which of the following is required to obtain a solicitation conviction?

   a. The person solicited must accept the offer.
   b. The solicitor must have specific intent.
   c. The solicitor and solicited must enter into a conspiracy.
   d. The person solicited must commit the crime.

24. At common law, the crime of attempt _____.

    a. did not exist
    b. had no specific intent element
    c. required some injury
    d. required that the defendant do the last proximate act

25. Physical proximity tests of attempt *actus reus* focus on _____.

    a. how close the defendant got to completing the crime
    b. whether a reasonable person would see that a crime is in progress
    c. whether the defendant is likely to cease the attempt
    d. how much of the defendant's intent is shown by action

26. The unequivocality test of attempt *actus reus* focuses on _____.

    a. whether the defendant is likely to give up the attempt
    b. how much remains to be done before completing the crime
    c. whether the defendant has taken substantial steps
    d. whether the defendant has started preparing for the crime

27. The Model Penal Code test of attempt *actus reus* focuses on _____.

    a. probable desistance and unequivocality
    b. steps taken by the defendant and unequivocality
    c. intent and steps taken by the defendant
    d. *res ipsa loquitur* and intent

28. According to the Model Penal Code, soliciting an innocent agent to commit the crime is _____.

    a. an attempted conspiracy
    b. an attempted solicitation
    c. an attempt
    d. a conspiracy

29. Unlike the early common law approach to attempt, the law today does not require _____.

    a. that any or partial harm be caused on inflicted
    b. any specific intent
    c. any general intent
    d. that there be any *actus reus*

30. At common law, an attempted capital offense such as robbery, murder, or burglary resulted in _____.

 a. execution
 b. sentencing to life in prison
 c. guilty of a non-capital felony
 d. guilty only of a misdemeanor

TRUE/FALSE

1. All inchoate offenses have a specific intent element.
 a. true
 b. false

2. Inchoate crimes are punished at the same level as the object or completed crime.
 a. true
 b. false

3. Attempt was not a crime at common law.
 a. true
 b. false

4. There are no such things as reckless, negligent, or strict liability attempts.
 a. true
 b. false

5. An attempt requires more than mere preparation to commit the crime.
 a. true
 b. false

6. The Model Penal Code definition of the *actus reus* of attempt is an example of the probable desistance approach.
 a. true
 b. false

7. Legal impossibility is a defense to the crime of attempt.
 a. true
 b. false

8. Factual impossibility is a valid defense to the crime of attempt.
 a. true
 b. false

9. The Model Penal Code *actus reus* of attempt involves substantial steps that strongly corroborate the actor's criminal purpose.
   a. true
   b. false

10. A person cannot be convicted of attempting to murder someone with a pistol if the pistol was, in fact, unloaded at the time.
    a. true
    b. false

11. To be a valid defense, the abandonment of an attempt must be voluntary.
    a. true
    b. false

12. In some jurisdictions, there are two act elements in the crime of conspiracy.
    a. true
    b. false

13. The offense of conspiracy is frequently criticized because of its vagueness.
    a. true
    b. false

14. The fact that one conspirator has been acquitted does not prevent the government from prosecuting the others for conspiracy.
    a. true
    b. false

15. In most modern conspiracy statutes, the criminal objective is usually limited to agreements to commit crimes.
    a. true
    b. false

16. RICO stands for Racketeer Influenced and Corrupt Organizations.
    a. true
    b. false

17. In some jurisdictions, the crime of solicitation is limited to solicitation to commit misdemeanors.
    a. true
    b. false

18. A solicitation that does not reach or is not heard by the intended recipient cannot be a crime.
    a. true
    b. false

19. To be criminal, a solicitation must be directed toward a specific individual.
    a. true
    b. false

20. The crime of solicitation is a strict liability crime.
    a. true
    b. false

21. In a wheel conspiracy, one or more defendants participate in every transaction.
    a. true
    b. false

22. A person can be guilty of conspiracy even though they do not know all of the others in the conspiracy.
    a. true
    b. false

23. The Model Penal Code definition of conspiracy includes an overt act element.
    a. true
    b. false

24. For the solicitor to be guilty of solicitation, the person solicited must accept the offer.
    a. true
    b. false

25. The primary purpose of requiring some overt act in some conspiracy statutes is to help identify who is involved in the conspiracy.
    a. true
    b. false

FILL-IN-THE-BLANK

1. Under the _____ test, an attempt has been committed when the person has gotten control of everything they need to complete the crime.

2. Abandonment is not a defense to attempt unless the abandonment is _____.

3. In some states, the second *actus reus* requirement is that there be a/n _____ act by one of the conspirators in pursuance of the conspiracy.

4. The term _____ means "the thing stands for itself."

5. _____ impossibility is not a valid defense to attempt.

6. The _____ test of attempt *actus reus* focuses on how close the defendant got to completing the crime.

7. Acts toward committing a crime that do not constitute an attempt are called _____.

8. In the _____ approach to conspiracy, a person can be guilty even though no one else in the conspiracy really agrees to commit the crime.

9. Under the _____ approach to attempt *actus reus*, the test is whether the acts confirm the intent.

10. _____ impossibility is a defense to attempt.

11. RICO means _____.

12. In a/n _____ conspiracy, one or more defendants participate in all transactions.

13. Of the inchoate offenses, only _____ is sometimes defined as having two act elements.

14. _____ can be thought of as the first half of a conspiracy.

15. The principle of _____ leads to the conclusion that legal impossibility is a defense to attempt.

ESSAY

1. Define, describe, compare, and contrast conspiracy, attempt and solicitation. Be sure to provide an example of each.

2. Discuss the various approaches to the *actus reus* of attempt. Provide an example of each.

3. Define, describe, compare, and contrast legal impossibility, factual impossibility, and abandonment as defenses to attempt.

4. Discuss how the law of conspiracy has changed since early common law? How have these changes dealt with modern, large-scale conspiracies.

5. How has the law of attempt changed since early common law?

CHAPTER 8 ANSWER KEY

Multiple Choice

1. c	2. a	3. d	4. b	5. b
6. c	7. b	8. d	9. d	10. c
11. b	12. c	13. a	14. d	15. c
16. d	17. d	18. d	19. a	20. b
21. d	22. a	23. a	24. c	25. a
26. a	27. c	28. c	29. a	30. a

True/False

1. T	2. F	3. F	4. T	5. T
6. F	7. T	8. F	9. T	10. F
11. T	12. T	13. T	14. T	15. T
16. T	17. F	18. F	19. F	20. F
21. T	22. T	23. T	24. F	25. F

Fill-in-the-Blank

1. indispensable element
2. voluntary
3. overt
4. *res ipsa loquitur*
5. Factual
6. physical proximity
7. mere preparation
8. unilateral
9. unequivocality
10. Legal
11. Racketeer Influenced and Corrupt Organizations
12. wheel
13. conspiracy
14. Solicitation
15. legality

CHAPTER 9
CRIMES AGAINST PERSONS I: HOMICIDE

LEARNING OBJECTIVES

After studying this chapter, students will understand that:

- Criminal homicide is different from all other crimes because of the finality of its result: the death of the victim.

- Most of the law of criminal homicide is about grading the seriousness of the offense.

- Grading murder into first and second degree is important because only first-degree murders qualify for the death penalty.

- Most criminal homicide statutes apply to corporations, but prosecutions are rare.

- The heart of voluntary manslaughter is an intentional, sudden killing triggered by an adequate provocation.

- Provocation isn't an excuse for criminal homicide: it only reduces the seriousness of the crime and the punishment to allow for human frailty.

KEY TERMS AND CONCEPTS

- **born-alive rule**—homicide law once said that to be a person, and therefore a homicide victim, a baby had to be "born alive" and capable of breathing and maintaining a heartbeat on its own; p. 275

- **feticide**—law defining when life begins for purposes of applying the law of criminal homicide; p. 277

- **murder**—intentionally causing the death of another person with "malice aforethought;" p. 277

- **manslaughter**—unlawful killing of another person without malice aforethought; p. 277

- **justifiable homicide**—killing in self-defense, capital punishment, and police use of deadly force; p. 278

- **excusable homicide**—accidental killings done by someone "not of sound memory and discretion" (insane and immature); p. 278

- **criminal homicide**—a homicide that's neither justified nor excused; p. 278

- **malice aforethought**—killing on purpose after planning it; p. 279

- **depraved-heart murder**—extremely reckless killing; p. 279

- **intent-to-cause-serious-bodily-injury**—murder when death results following acts triggered by the intent to inflict serious bodily injury short of death; p. 280

- **express malice aforethought**—intentional killings planned in advance; p. 280

- **implied malice aforethought**—killings that weren't intentional or planned but still resulted from the intention to do harm; p. 280

- **murder *actus reus***—causing the death of a person; p. 281

- **murder *mens rea***—the purposeful, knowing, reckless, or negligent killing of a person; p. 282

- **capital case**—death penalty cases in death penalty states and "mandatory life sentence without parole" cases in non-death penalty states; p. 283

- **bifurcation**—a mandate that the death penalty decision be made in two phases: a trial to determine guilt and a second separate proceeding, after a finding of guilt, to consider the aggravating factors for, and mitigating factors against, capital punishment; p. 283

- **criteria for decision (in death penalty cases)**—must be limited by the criteria established and announced *before* the decision to sentence the defendant to death but includes aggravating factors for and mitigating factors against imposing death; p. 283

- **specific-intent-plus-real-premeditation-deliberation definition**—the law looks at three areas to determine whether a killing was premeditated and deliberate: signs of planning, motive, and deliberate method in the killing; p. 286

- **equivalent-of-specific-intent definition**—some courts define a willful, premeditated, deliberate killing as the same as specific intent, which may render the difference between first- and second-degree murder meaningless; p. 287

- **first-degree murder**—premeditated, deliberate killings and other particularly heinous capital murders; p. 292

- **second-degree murder**—a catchall offense including killings that are neither manslaughter nor first-degree murder; unintentional killings; p. 295

- **felony murder**—unintentional deaths that occur during the commission of felonies; p. 300

- **third-party exception**—defense to felony murder that someone other than the felon caused the death during the commission of a felony; p. 302

- **resisting-victim exception**—exception to the third-party exception to felony murder, in which the defendant can be charged with the killing of his accomplice, which was committed by the resisting victim; p. 302

- **inherently dangerous felony approach**—courts look at the felony in the abstract—if a felony *can* be committed in a way that's *not* dangerous to life, even if it was committed in a dangerous way, then it's not inherently dangerous; p. 302

- **case-by-case approach**—the facts and circumstances surrounding the way the felony was committed in the particular case, not the elements of the crime in the abstract, may be considered to determine whether it was dangerous to human life; p. 303

- **involuntary manslaughter**—criminal homicides caused either by recklessness or gross criminal negligence; p. 311

- **adequate provocation**—the circumstance element in voluntary manslaughter that is the trigger that sets off the sudden killing of another person; acts that qualify as reducing murder to manslaughter; p. 311

- **objective test of cooling-off-time**—in voluntary manslaughter, the element of whether, in similar circumstances, a reasonable person would have had time to cool off; p. 312

- **last-straw rule**—a smoldering resentment or pent-up rage resulting from earlier insults or humiliating events, culminating in a triggering event that, by itself, might be insufficient to provoke the deadly act; p. 313

- **extreme mental or emotional disturbance**—a defense that reduces criminal homicide to manslaughter if emotional disturbance provides a reasonable explanation for the defendant's actions; p. 313

- **paramour rule**—a husband who caught his wife in the act of adultery had adequate provocation to kill and could reduce criminal homicide to voluntary manslaughter; p. 314

- **involuntary manslaughter**—criminal homicides caused either by recklessness or gross negligence and resulting in the unconscious creation of substantial and unjustifiable risks; p. 317

- **criminal negligence manslaughter**—includes the mental elements of both recklessness and negligence; p. 317

- **unlawful act manslaughter**—sometimes called "misdemeanor manslaughter," it's involuntary manslaughter based on deaths that take place during the commission of another crime; p. 321

- **unlawful act**—include everything from committing felonies, misdemeanors, and even traffic violations, city ordinances, administrative crimes, and non-criminal wrongs, such as civil trespass and other torts; p. 321

CHAPTER OUTLINE

I. Criminal Homicide in Context
   A. Criminal homicide is relatively rare.
   B. Criminal homicide is the most serious of all felonies known to our law.
   C. Criminal homicide is divided into two categories: murder and manslaughter.
   D. How we classify a killing determines what punishment should be inflicted upon the offender.

II. The Meaning of "Person" or "Human Being"
Defining the beginning and end of life is controversial and differs among jurisdictions (some include fetal murder and brain death).
   A. **When does life begin?** Homicide law has generally followed a born-alive rule.
      1. Born-alive rule
         a. *Case: People v. Chavez* (exception to the rule)
         b. *Case: Keeler v. Superior Court*
         c. *Case: State v. Cotton*
      2. Feticide
   B. **When does life end?**
      1. The determination that life has ended has evolved from the cessation of the heart beating, the lungs breathing, to "brain death"
      2. The development of artificial life support has complicated homicide law and introduced legal, ethical, and moral complications.

III. Murder
   A. The History of Murder Law
      1. English common-law murder recognized three forms of homicide:
         a. Justifiable homicide
         b. Excusable homicide
         c. Criminal homicide
      2. Murder defined by Coke in the early 1600s—"When a person of sound memory and discretion, unlawffuly [sic] killeth any reasonable creature in being and under the king's peace, with malice aforethought, either express or implied."

3. Blackstone's definition, 1796:
    a. Malice aforethought, express or implied: with specific intent or killing on purpose, with some bad will; planned in advance
    b. Reasonable creature meant someone already born alive

B. **The Elements of Murder**—The elements of criminal homicide are act, intent, concurrence, causation, and harm.
    1. At common law, murder was the unlawful killing of another with malice aforethought.
        a. Express malice aforethought: fits original meaning of murder—intentional killings planned in advance
    2. Historically, the concept of "malice aforethought" was expanded to include implied malice. It consisted of five mental states—the specific intent to do one of the following:
        a. Kill another person (express malice aforethought)
        b. Seriously injure another person
        c. Commit specified dangerous felonies
        d. Forcibly resist a lawful arrest
        e. Create a higher than criminally reckless risk of death or serious bodily injury (depraved-heart murder)
    3. **Murder *actus reus***—taking the life of or causing the death of another person (live human being)
    Defining the beginning and end of life is controversial and differs among jurisdictions (some include fetal murder and brain death).
        a. Includes all voluntary actions such as poisoning, striking, starving, and drowning
        b. Also includes voluntary omissions
        c. How the murderer kills doesn't matter in most cases (but could aggravate it)
    4. **Murder *mens rea***—varies over time and from jurisdiction, but typically:
        1. Purposely (intentionally)
        2. Knowingly
        3. Recklessly
        4. Negligently
    5. Causation—acts that set in motion a chain of events that amount to cause in fact or legal cause of the death of another.
    6. Criminal harm resulting in the death of another

C. **The Kinds and Degrees of Murder**—Murder is the most serious form of criminal homicide.
    1. Originally murder was never divided into degrees, all murders were capital offenses.
    2. Dividing murder into degrees was a product of not wishing to execute all persons convicted of criminal homicide, following the tradition of letting judges mitigate penalties by use of "benefit of clergy."
    3. Many statutes followed the same common-law scheme in dividing up premeditated and felony murder.

4. The Model Penal code doesn't use the degrees, but does divide murder according to mental attitude.
5. Today, most jurisdictions have two degrees of homicide (some have three).

D. First-degree Murder
1. **Death Penalty**—discretionary in all states authorizing the death penalty
    a. Highly complex
    b. Several constitutional limitations
        (1) Mandatory death sentences are banned.
        (2) Unguided discretionary death penalty sentences are banned.
        (3) Mitigating factors are required.
        (4) Additional aggravating factors are allowed.
    c. Most states have adopted MPC's recommendation of bifurcation and a criteria for decision.
2. **First-degree murder *mens rea*** (capital offense in states with the death penalty)
    a. Premeditated, deliberate killings
    b. Atrocious, brutal, or cruel murders (in capital cases)
    c. Specific-intent-plus-real-premeditation-deliberation definition
    d. Equivalent-of-specific-intent definition
    e. *Case: Byford v. State*
    f. *Case: State v. Thompson*
    g. *Case: State v. Snowden*
3. **First-degree murder *actus reus***
    a. Generally the manner of killing doesn't matter.
    b. Manner could be critical if it could be a capital offense.
    c. Some states have statutes making heinous, atrocious, and cruel first-degree murder capital offenses.
    d. *Case: Henyard v. State*
    e. *Case: Commonwealth v. Golston*
    f. *Case: Duest v. State*

E. Second-degree murder
1. Divide murder for purposes of determining capital and non-capital punishment.
2. Divide between intentional and unintentional murder—second-degree murders are unintentional murders.
    a. **Depraved-heart murder**
        (1) Unintentional killing without premeditation
        (2) Killings resulting from the intent to do serious bodily injury
        (3) Killings resulting from the resisting of lawful arrest
        (4) Killings that occur during the commission of felonies
        (5) *Case: People v. Protopappas*
        (6) *Case: People v. Thomas*
    b. **Felony murder**—unintentional death that occurs while committing dangerous felonies
        (1) Intent to commit the underlying crime satisfies the *mens rea* of felony murder.

(2) Felony murder has three goals:
    (a) Deterrence
    (b) Reduce violence
    (c) Punish wrongdoers
(3) Four states have abolished it.
(4) When someone besides the defendant caused the death
    (a) Third-party exception prevents felony murder conviction.
    (b) Resisting victim exception allows felony murder conviction.
(5) *Case: People v. Phillips*
(6) *Case: State v. Harrison*
(7) *Case: State v. Stewart*

  F. **Corporation murders**
    1. Corporations can legally commit murder.
    2. Usually, prosecutions of corporations for criminal homicide don't succeed.
    3. Examples: Fort Pinto; Autumn Hills Convalescent Centers
    4. *Case: People v. O'Neil*

IV. **Manslaughter** is divided into two types.
  A. Two types: voluntary or involuntary
  B. Elements of **voluntary manslaughter**
    1. *Actus reus*—taking the life or causing the death of another person
    2. *Mens rea*—intent to kill or cause serious bodily harm
    3. **Adequate provocation**
      a. Is a circumstance element
      b. Occurs in the sudden heat of passion before there was a reasonable time for the passion to cool off.
        (1) Objective test of cooling off
        (2) Case: *State v. Flory*
      c. Caused both the passion and the killing
      d. Is specified by law
        (1) Fighting (mutual combat)
        (2) Assault and battery
        (3) Trespass
        (4) Adultery (paramour rule)
      e. Response must be reasonable to ordinary people.
      f. Never consists of words
    4. **Causation**—the acts that triggered the chain of events that led to the death
    5. Result—the death of another
    6. **Provocation by Words**
      a. Last-straw rule
      b. Words can never provoke rule (most states)
        (1) *Dennis v. State*

       7. **Provocation by Intimates**
          a. Paramour rule
          b. *Case: Commonwealth v. Schnopps*
          c. *Case: People v. Washington*
  C. **Involuntary manslaughter** is the killing of another person unintentionally.
      1. **Criminal Negligence/Vehicular/Firearms Manslaughter**
          a. Requires the *mens rea* of either criminal recklessness or criminal negligence
          b. Occurs during the commission of unlawful acts (like reckless or negligent driving)
          c. *Case: State v. Mays*
      2. **Unlawful act manslaughter**
          a. Most jurisdictions no longer recognize the misdemeanor-manslaughter or unlawful act manslaughter doctrines.

CHAPTER SUMMARY

Criminal homicides are different from all other crimes because of the finality of the result—the death of the victim. Because of the seriousness of the harm and the penalty, this is probably the most complex area of substantive criminal law. Although the definitions vary from state to state, there are many common principles. All criminal homicides involve the killing of another person. The *mens rea* can include knowingly, intentionally, purposely, recklessly, and negligently. The *mens rea* must trigger the act, and the act must cause the death. The causation element has two components: cause in fact and legal cause.

The law of homicide has its origins in the common law. Early on, there were only three types of homicide: justifiable, excusable, and criminal. A justifiable murder was not punishable if the defendant could establish a justification such as self-defense. An excusable murder was not criminal if the defendant could establish an excuse such as an accident.

Murder was defined as killing with malice aforethought. The crime of murder was expanded by creating implied malice situations, such as the depraved-heart and felony murder. The common law also created the crime of voluntary manslaughter, which involved an intentional killing during the heat of passion.

The *actus reus* of criminal homicide is killing another person. Today, in many jurisdictions, a fetus can be the victim of a criminal homicide. Advances in medical science have changed the definition of death. Brain death qualifies as death even though the person may be able to continue breathing.

The *mens rea* of criminal homicide is typically intentionally, knowingly, recklessly, or negligently (criminal negligence). There are, however, other types of murders. For instance, the intent to commit a qualifying felony substitutes for the intent to kill in felony murder. Many states have limited the felony murder doctrine to violent or dangerous felonies

Most of the law of criminal homicide is about grading the offense according to the elements of *mens rea*, *actus reus*, or mitigating or aggravating circumstances. The common law did not recognize degrees of murder. Pennsylvania was the first state to divide murder into two degrees. Most states have four basic types of murder: first-degree murder, second-degree murder, voluntary manslaughter and involuntary manslaughter. Grading murder into first- and second-degree is important because in some states only first-degree (or capital) murders qualify for the death penalty (or prison for life without parole in states without the death penalty). Second-degree murder is typically an unpremeditated but intentional killing.

Most murder statutes apply to corporations. However, in most cases, liability doesn't extend beyond the rare prosecution for involuntary manslaughter in outrageous cases.

A voluntary manslaughter is an intentional, sudden killing triggered by an adequate provocation. Provocation isn't an excuse for criminal homicide; it only reduces the punishment to allow for human weaknesses. Most jurisdictions have both objective and subjective requirements for the elements of voluntary manslaughter. Only certain types of provocation are deemed legally adequate. Usually, these are mutual combat, assault and battery, trespass, and adultery. Words alone are, in many states, not deemed an adequate provocation. However, in other states following the "last-straw rule," words may be sufficient provocation. Catching a spouse in the act of adultery is generally recognized as an adequate provocation. Further, the killer must not have cooled off from the sudden passion. If the killer did cool off, it is an intentional murder and not a voluntary manslaughter. Specifically, the elements of voluntary manslaughter are as follows. The *actus reus* is killing of another person. The *mens rea* is intent to kill or inflict serious bodily injury. The circumstances are sudden heat of passion flowing from an adequate provocation (or honest but unreasonable belief that killing was necessary in self-defense). The acts must cause the death of another.

Involuntary manslaughter is the least blameworthy form of criminal homicide. It involves unintentional (reckless or negligent) killing. Recklessness involves conscious creation of a serous and unjustifiable risk. Negligence involves unknowing creation of a substantial and unjustifiable risk.

The common law and early statutes recognized a form of involuntary manslaughter that involved an intentional killing during the course of committing a misdemeanor or an unlawful act. Most jurisdictions have severely limited or abolished this form of involuntary manslaughter.

PRACTICE TEST BANK

MULTIPLE CHOICE

1. Most states have _____.

    a. abolished felony murder
    b. limited the types of felonies which qualify to violent or dangerous felonies
    c. made felony murder a form of involuntary manslaughter
    d. made felony murder a form of voluntary manslaughter

2. Implied malice includes intent to _____.

    a. commit any felony or misdemeanor
    b. commit a dangerous misdemeanor
    c. commit any illegal act
    d. inflict serious bodily harm

3. The degree of murder or type of homicide is determined by the *actus reus*, special circumstances, and the _____.
    a. concurrence
    b. act
    c. harm
    d. *mens rea*

4. The term "homicide" is usually defined as _____.

    a. killing another live human being
    b. a criminal offense where the victim dies
    c. a murder or a suicide
    d. a murder

5. A murder that was perpetrated by means of planned, intentional poisoning of two elderly parents to collect life insurance would be a/n _____.

    a. second-degree murder
    b. involuntary manslaughter
    c. first-degree murder
    d. voluntary manslaughter

6. An unintentional criminal homicide that resulted from a conscious risk of harm greater than recklessness is usually termed a _____.

   a. felony murder
   b. depraved-heart murder
   c. voluntary manslaughter
   d. excusable homicide

7. With regard to cooling off for voluntary manslaughter, assuming the defendant did, in fact, honestly not cool off, most courts would also then apply a/n _____ reasonable person test.

   a. objective
   b. overt
   c. lenient
   d. subjective

8. Although it is no longer the case, a few states went further than most with the paramour rule. In these states, wife killings during adultery were _____.

   a. justifiable homicides
   b. voluntary manslaughter
   c. involuntary manslaughter
   d. depraved-heart murders

9. Originally, the benefit of the paramour rule could be claimed by _____.

   a. wives only
   b. both husbands and wives
   c. the spouse's paramour only
   d. husbands only

10. Conscious creation of a substantial and unjustifiable risk is _____.

    a. negligence
    b. gross negligence
    c. recklessness
    d. criminal negligence

11. If the defendant accidentally killed the store clerk during an armed robbery this would be a/n _____.

    a. felony murder
    b. excusable homicide
    c. involuntary manslaughter
    d. depraved heart murder

12. Common-law judges expanded the original definition of murder by creating the concept of _____ malice aforethought.

    a. express
    b. constitutive
    c. implied
    d. latent

13. At early common law, there was only one type of criminal homicide, homicide _____.

    a. committed during a felony
    b. that was neither excused nor justified
    c. depraved-heart murder
    d. in the form of manslaughter

14. As the common law developed, murder was distinguished from manslaughter in that murder required _____.

    a. malice aforethought
    b. adequate provocation
    c. heat of passion
    d. no *actus reus*

15. In 1794, _____ was the first state to separate murder into two degrees.

    a. Virginia
    b. New York
    c. Pennsylvania
    d. Massachusetts

16. As compared to traditional murder law, the felony murder rule doesn't require _____.

    a. malice aforethought or an intent or purpose to kill
    b. intent to commit a felony
    c. an *actus reus*
    d. that the defendant's acts cause the victim's death

17. The common-law crime of manslaughter was eventually divided into two separate types, _____.

    a. voluntary and involuntary
    b. deliberate and premeditated
    c. first and second degree
    d. with implied or express malice

18. The main difference between voluntary and involuntary manslaughter is that in involuntary manslaughter, the killing is _____.

    a. unintentional
    b. totally unforeseeable
    c. with implied malice
    d. with express malice

19. If the defendant killed another in an honest but unreasonable belief that the killing was necessary for self-defense, this would be the crime of _____.

    a. involuntary manslaughter
    b. voluntary manslaughter
    c. excusable homicide
    d. justifiable homicide

20. Voluntary manslaughter involves intentionally killing another in the sudden heat of passion which _____.

    a. was caused by a legally recognized adequate provocation
    b. was caused by a mental disease or defect
    c. caused the actor to be reckless
    d. gave the actor time to cool off

21. In most states, which of the following is not deemed to be a legally adequate provocation for voluntary manslaughter?

    a. verbal provocation
    b. mutual combat
    c. adultery by spouse
    d. assault and battery

22. The *mens rea* of involuntary manslaughter is usually _____.

    a. recklessly or negligently
    b. intentionally
    c. deliberate and premeditated
    d. implied malice

23. Which of the following is typically an aggravating circumstance that will justify infliction of the death penalty?

    a. torture of victim
    b. victim attempted to defend themselves
    c. victim was related to offender
    d. victim was a stranger

24. Over time, the substantive law of criminal homicide has _____.

    a. become more complex
    b. come to exclude corporations from liability for criminal homicide
    c. come to include more capital offenses
    d. allowed numerous blameworthy individuals to avoid punishment

25. Unlawful act manslaughter is sometimes also referred to as _____.

    a. voluntary manslaughter
    b. misdemeanor manslaughter
    c. felony murder
    d. depraved-heart murder

26. The _____ element of all homicides is the killing of another person.

    a. *mens rea*
    b. *actus reus*
    c. circumstances
    d. concurrence

27. In the first statute creating two degrees of murder (1794), (and in some current statutes), second-degree murder was defined as _____.

    a. a deliberate and premeditated killing
    b. a killing with malice aforethought
    c. intentional killing during the course of rape, robbery, etc.
    d. any murder that is not a first-degree murder

28. Felony murder requires intent to _____.

    a. kill
    b. inflict serious bodily injury
    c. inflict any bodily injury
    d. commit a felony

Study Guide

29. Felony murders are usually _____.

    a. first- or second-degree murders
    b. second-degree murders or voluntary manslaughters
    c. voluntary or involuntary manslaughters
    d. involuntary manslaughters or negligent homicides

30. In most jurisdictions, second-degree murder is a murder _____.

    a. with malice aforethought
    b. done intentionally but without premeditation
    c. done with premeditation but not intentionally
    d. done with recklessness aforethought

TRUE/FALSE

1. Second-degree murder is generally an intentional but unpremeditated murder.
    a. true
    b. false

2. No corporation has ever been charged with a criminal homicide.
    a. true
    b. false

3. A defendant who cools off after the provocation and then intentionally kills is guilty of voluntary manslaughter.
    a. true
    b. false

4. Reckless or negligent criminal homicides are usually termed involuntary manslaughter.
    a. true
    b. false

5. Recklessness has both objective and subjective components.
    a. true
    b. false

6. At common law, murder was divided into first, second, and third degrees.
    a. true
    b. false

7. In some jurisdictions, murders that include aggravating circumstances (torture, heinous, atrocious, or cruel) are capital offenses.
    a. true
    b. false

8. The Eighth Amendment requires case-by-case consideration of aggravating and mitigating factors before the death penalty can be imposed.
    a. true
    b. false

9. Manslaughter was not a common-law crime.
    a. true
    b. false

10. Insulting gestures or words and racial slurs are adequate legal provocation for manslaughter.
    a. true
    b. false

11. At common law, a criminal homicide committed with malice aforethought is a murder.
    a. true
    b. false

12. All felony murders are intentional homicides.
    a. true
    b. false

13. Not all homicides are criminal.
    a. true
    b. false

14. Corporations cannot be guilty of criminal homicide.
    a. true
    b. false

15. Voluntary manslaughter is a form of unintentional homicide.
    a. true
    b. false

16. The trend in the law is to expand the illegal act manslaughter rule.
    a. true
    b. false

17. In most jurisdictions today, any type of felony will qualify for the felony murder rule.
    a. true
    b. false

18. Most, if not all, jurisdictions recognize brain death as a legal death.
    a. true
    b. false

Study Guide

19. An accidental killing, involving no fault on the actor's part, would be an excusable homicide.
    a. true
    b. false

20. In some states, a person can be guilty of the crime of killing a fetus.
    a. true
    b. false

21. A homicide committed in valid self-defense would be a justifiable homicide.
    a. true
    b. false

22. The common-law term "aforethought" refers to planning in advance.
    a. true
    b. false

23. The *actus reus* of homicide is killing another person or human being.
    a. true
    b. false

24. Most, if not all, involuntary manslaughters have two *actus reus* elements.
    a. true
    b. false

25. At common law, life (or becoming a person) began at conception.
    a. true
    b. false

FILL-IN-THE-BLANK

1. For a felony to qualify for the felony murder rule, most states require that the felony be a violent or _____ felony.

2. One of the most highly publicized cases of alleged corporate criminal homicides involved the _____ automobile.

3. A valid self-defense killing is a form of _____ homicide.

4. At common law, murder was killing someone with _____.

5. Insulting gestures and words are generally not legally adequate provocation for purposes of _____ manslaughter.

6. An accidental killing can be a murder and not an excusable homicide under the _____ murder rule.

7. The *mens rea* for involuntary manslaughter is recklessness or _____.

8. The unintentional killing form of manslaughter is _____ manslaughter.

9. An intentional killing that occurred under circumstances of imperfect self-defense is a _____ manslaughter.

10. The _____ rule is an exception to the felony murder rule.

11. A killing is with _____ if it is intentional and without excuse or justification.

12. The most serious form of murder today is capital or _____ murder.

13. Conscious creation of a serious and substantial risk is called _____.

14. Creating serious and substantial risks but not being aware of it is called _____.

15. An unintentional death caused by driving while intoxicated would be a form of _____ manslaughter.

ESSAY

1. Compare and contrast first-degree murder and second-degree murder.

2. Discuss the history and development of the felony murder rule. Compare and contrast the California approach to inherently dangerous felonies to the Rhode Island approach.

3. Compare and contrast voluntary and involuntary manslaughter.

4. Compare and contrast justifiable, excusable, and criminal homicide.

5. Discuss the development and history of common-law murder and manslaughter.

CHAPTER 9 ANSWER KEY

Multiple Choice

1. b	2. d	3. d	4. a	5. c
6. b	7. a	8. a	9. d	10. c
11. a	12. c	13. b	14. a	15. c
16. a	17. a	18. a	19. b	20. a
21. a	22. a	23. a	24. a	25. b
26. b	27. d	28. d	29. a	30. b

True/False

1. T	2. F	3. F	4. T	5. T
6. F	7. T	8. T	9. F	10. F
11. T	12. F	13. T	14. F	15. F
16. F	17. F	18. T	19. T	20. T
21. T	22. T	23. T	24. F	25. F

Fill-in-the-Blank

1. dangerous
2. Ford Pinto
3. justifiable
4. malice
5. voluntary
6. felony
7. negligence
8. involuntary
9. voluntary
10. third-party exception
11. malice
12. first-degree
13. recklessness
14. negligence
15. involuntary

CHAPTER 10
CRIMES AGAINST PERSONS II:
CRIMINAL SEXUAL CONDUCT, BODILY INJURY, AND PERSONAL RESTRAINT

LEARNING OBJECTIVES

After studying this chapter, students will understand that:

- Crimes against persons boil down to four types: taking a life, unwanted sexual invasions, bodily injury, and personal restraint.

- Rape is regarded by the law and society as second only to murder as the most serious crime.

- Under consensual circumstances, behaviors connected with sexual assault are legal, healthy, and desired.

- Criminal law originally recognized two types of sex offenses: rape and sodomy.

- The vast majority of rape victims are raped by men they know.

- Aggravated rape and unarmed acquaintance rape are two classes of rape used in prosecuting defendants accused of rape.

- Until the 1970s, rape was a capital offense.

- The 1970s and 1980s gave way to reform in modern criminal sexual conduct and assault statutes; gender-neutral sex offenses were incorporated, including unwanted sexual penetrations and contacts.

- Most states recognize four degrees of criminal sexual assault or conduct.

- Force and resistance are necessary elements to convict a defendant accused of rape. Actual force isn't required to satisfy the force requirement; the threat of force is enough.

- No resistance is required if victims were incapacitated at the time of the assault by intoxication, mental deficiency, or insanity.

- Rape is a general-intent crime; defendants intended to commit the act defined in the crime. Courts vary on whether consent is a defense to sexual assault of adult victims; some recognize negligent mistake, other require reckless mistake, and some adopt a strict liability approach.

Chapter 10: Crimes Against Persons II: Criminal Sexual Conduct—Bodily Injury, and Personal Restraint

- Critics argue that rape is too serious a charge and the penalties are too severe to allow convictions based on negligent, reckless, or no-fault mistakes.

- Statutory rape consists of having sex with minors; force isn't a necessary element because of the immaturity of the victim. Most states define statutory rape as a strict liability crime with regard to the element of the victim's age.

- Assault and battery, although combined in many modern statutes, are two separate crimes. Battery is an unwanted and unjustified offensive touching in which body contact is the central element; assault is either an attempted or a threatened battery and requires no physical contact.

- Stalking, however ancient in practice, is a relatively new *crime*.

- Stalking leads to depression, substance abuse, phobias, anxiety, obsessive-compulsive behaviors, and dissociative disorders in the victim.

- The right locomotion allows people to come and go as they please; kidnapping and false imprisonment violate that right.

KEY TERMS AND CONCEPTS

- **common-law rape**—intentional, forced, heterosexual vaginal penetration by a man with a woman not his wife; p. 330

- **common-law sodomy**—anal intercourse between two males; p. 331

- **sexual assault statutes**—expanded the definition of sex offenses to embrace a wide range of nonconsensual penetrations and contacts; p. 331

- **criminal sexual conduct statutes**—expanded the definition of sex offenses to embrace a wide range of nonconsensual penetrations and contact; p. 331

- **aggravated rape (first degree)**—rape committed with a weapon, by more than one person, or causing serious physical injury to the victim; p. 331

- **unarmed acquaintance rape**—nonconsensual sex between people who know each other; rape involving dates, lovers, neighbors, co-workers, employers, and so on; p. 331

- **corroboration rule**—element in rape that the prosecution had to prove rape by the testimony of witnesses other than the victim; p. 332

- **rape shield statutes**—statutes that prohibit introducing evidence of victims' past sexual conduct; p. 332

- **prompt-reporting rule**—rape victims have to report the rape soon after it occurs; p. 332

- **marital rape exception**—legally, husbands can't rape their wives; p. 333

- **rape**—intentional sexual penetration by force without consent; p. 334

- **rape** *actus reus*—the act of sexual penetration; p. 335

- **force and resistance rule**—victims had to prove to the courts they didn't consent to rape by demonstrating that they resisted the force of the rapist; p. 335

- **utmost resistance rule**—the requirement that rape victims must use all the physical strength they have to prevent penetration; p. 335

- **reasonable resistance rule (in rape)**—the amount of force required to repel rapists to show non-consent in rape prosecutions; p. 336

- **extrinsic force**—requires some force, in addition to the amount needed to accomplish the penetration; p. 337

- **intrinsic force**—requires only the amount of force necessary to accomplish the penetration; p. 337

- **threat-of-force requirement**—prosecution must prove a sexual assault victim feared imminent bodily harm and that the fear was reasonable; p. 343

- **fraud in the fact (in rape)**—when a rapist fraudulently convinces his victim that the act she consented to was something other than sexual intercourse; p. 343

- **fraud in the inducement**—the fraud is in the benefits promised, not in the act; p. 344

- **honest and reasonable mistake rule**—a negligence mental element in rape cases in which the defendant argues that he honestly, but mistakenly, believed the victim consented to sex; p. 344

- **recklessness requirement (regarding consent in rape)**—adopted by some states in rape cases; it requires that the defendant has to be aware that there's a risk the victim hasn't consented to sexual intercourse; p. 345

- **statutory rape**—to have carnal knowledge of a person under the age of consent whether or not accomplished by force; p. 346

- **reasonable mistake of age**—a defense to statutory rape in California and Alaska, if the defendant reasonably believed his victim was over the age of consent; p. 346

- **simple rape (second degree)**—rape without aggravated circumstances; p. 347

- **battery**—unwanted and unjustified offensive touching; p. 347

- **assault**—an attempt to commit a battery or intentionally putting another in fear; p. 347

- **stalking**—intentionally scaring another person by following, tormenting, or harassing; p. 347

- **attempted battery assault**—consists of having the specific intent to commit a battery and taking substantial steps toward carrying it out, without actually completing the attempt; p. 348

- **threatened battery assault**—sometimes called the crime of "intentional scaring," it requires only that actors intend to frighten their victims, thus expanding assault beyond attempted battery; p. 348

- **conditional threats**—not enough to satisfy the *mens rea* of assault because they're not immediate; p. 349

- **subjective and objective fear test**—asks if the defendant's acts "induce[d] fear in the victim," and if the acts would "cause a reasonable person to fear;" p. 352

- **subjective fear only test**—asks, was the victim actually afraid? p. 352

- **objective fear only test**—asks, would a reasonable person be afraid? p. 352

- **intent-to-instill-fear test**—asks, did the actor intend to instill fear? p. 352

- **cyberstalking**—the use of the internet, e-mail, or other electronic communications devices to stalk another person through threatening behavior; p. 352

- **right of locomotion**—the right to come and go without restraint; p. 356

- **kidnapping**—taking and carrying away another person with intent to deprive the other person of personal liberty; p. 356

- **asportation**—the carrying away of another's property; p. 357

- **false imprisonment**—the heart of the crime is depriving others of their personal liberty; p. 361

CHAPTER OUTLINE

I. Other than homicide, there are three kinds of crimes against persons—sexual, bodily injury, and restraint.
    A. Sex offenses *(e.g.*, rape)
    B. Bodily injury crimes *(e.g.*, assault)
    C. Personal restraint crimes *(e.g.*, kidnapping and false imprisonment)

II. Sex Offenses—Forcible rape was an offense at common law but has been modified greatly since then. The criminal justice system has struggled in dealing with acquaintance rapes and sexual assaults against men.
    A. **The history of rape law**
        1. Originally, only narrowly defined rape and sodomy
            a. Rape—forced heterosexual vaginal penetration of a woman not married to the rapist
            b. Sodomy—anal intercourse between males
        2. The elements of common-law rape
            a. Intentional vaginal intercourse
            b. Between a man and a woman not his wife
            c. Achieved by force or threat of serious bodily harm
            d. Without the woman's consent
        3. Victims could testify against rapists, but the woman's credibility depended on three conditions that were difficult (if not impossible) to prove:
            a. Her chastity
            b. Whether she reported the rape promptly
            c. Whether the rape was corroborated by other testimony
    B. **Criminal Sexual Conduct Statutes**
        1. Rape and related sex offense law reforms (1970s–80s)
            a. Changes in prosecution procedures
            b. Abolished the corroboration rule
            c. Relaxed the prompt-reporting rule
            d. Banned introduction of evidence of the victim's past sexual conduct through rape shield laws
            e. Changes in the definition of rape and related sex offenses
                (1) Marital rape exception (husbands can't rape wives) abolished in some states.
        2. Sexual offenses consolidated into one statute.
            a. All nonconsensual sexual penetrations and contacts included.=
            b. Sex offenses made gender-neutral.
            c. Seriousness of offense divided into several degrees, graded by:
                (1) Penetration (more serious) and contact (less serious)
                (2) Use of force (more serious)
                (3) Physical injury aggravates crime
                (4) Gang rapes are more serious.

C. **The elements of modern rape law**
   1. **Rape *actus reus*** — two parts
      a. Sexual penetration, however slight
      b. Force and resistance standard — focused on the woman's consent
         (1) Utmost resistance standard (1600s–1950s) — Victims had to prove by resistance to the utmost that they didn't consent.
         (2) Reasonable resistance standard (1950s–70s) — Amount of required resistance depended on the circumstances of each case.
         (3) Many new statutes have dropped the resistance requirement.
            (a) Stranger rape, resistance isn't really an issue
            (b) Acquaintance rape, resistance is critical
         (4) *Case: Jones v. State*
      c. By force or threat of force — Force
         (1) "Intrinsic" in some jurisdictions — only the amount of physical exertion needed to achieve penetration in nonconsensual sex
         (2) "Extrinsic" in some jurisdictions — some force in addition to the amount of exertion needed to achieve nonconsensual penetration
         (3) *Case: Commonwealth v. Berkowitz*
         (4) *Case: State in the Interest of M.T.S.*
      d. By force or threat of force — Threat of Force
         (1) Subjective fear requirement
         (2) Objective fear requirement
      e. Resistance and danger to victim
         (1) 1970s-80s research indicated resistance may endanger victims
         (2) Later research reflects that earlier findings were flawed.
            (a) Overrepresented stranger rape — violent convicted rapists
            (b) Acquaintance rape outnumber stranger rapes, and resistance usually succeeds with acquaintances.
            (c) Initial rapist violence provokes victim resistance rather than the other way around.
         (3) No force or threat required if victim is insane or tricked.
            (a) Fraud in the fact — is rape
            (b) Fraud in the inducement — isn't rape
   2. **Rape *mens rea*** — Rape is a general-intent crime: defendant must intend to commit the act of forcible sexual penetration.
      a. Different states of mind surrounding non-consent
      b. Mistakes can be either reckless, negligent, or no-fault (strict liability) mistakes
      c. Strict liability with respect to intent to use force
         (1) *Case: Commonwealth v. Fischer*
      d. Negligent mistake — honest but reasonable mistake rule
         (1) *Case: People v. Mayberry*

e. Reckless mistake—Defendant has to be aware that there is a risk the victim hasn't consented to the intercourse.
: : (1) *Case: Regina v. Morgan* (England)
: 3. Circumstance—non-consent by the victim
: : a. Formal law—state has to prove non-consent beyond a reasonable doubt.
: : b. Informal practice—defendants raise consent by the victim as a defense.
: : c. Consent doesn't have to be in writing.
D. **Statutory rape**
: 1. Victim's immaturity substitutes for the element of consent.
: 2. Strict liability as to age in most states
: 3. A few states allow a defense of reasonable mistake of age.
E. **Grading Degrees of Rape**
: 1. Simple rape
: 2. Aggravated rape is rape with injury, a stranger, another crime, an armed rapist, multiple rapists, or a minor victim.

III. **Bodily injury crimes** involve offensive touching or bodily harm.
: A. **Battery** is unwanted and unjustified offensive touching; assault is either an attempted or threatened battery.
: B. The elements of battery
: : 1. *Actus reus*
: : : a. Unlawful touching
: : : b. Only unauthorized offensive touching (parents and law enforcement officers are authorized)
: : 2. *Mens rea* varies as to whether it requires purposely, knowingly, recklessly, or negligently offensive touching.
: C. Grading the seriousness depends on:
: : 1. The degree of injury—mere touching, minor injury, or serious injury
: : 2. The circumstances of the touching

: D. **Assault** elements
: : 1. Assault requires no touching
: : 2. Kinds:
: : : a. Attempted battery assault elements—having the specific intent to commit battery and taking steps to complete it.
: : : b. Threatened battery assault elements—intentionally scaring the victim.
: : 3. Victim awareness
: : : a. Not important in attempted battery because the offense focuses on the physical injury.
: : : b. Indispensable in threatened battery because the offense focuses on fear of the victim.
: : 4. Conditional threats aren't enough for threatened battery assault.
: E. The Model assault and battery statute
: : 1. Part of the Model Penal Code
: : 2. Integrates, rationalizes, and grades assault and battery
: : 3. Takes into account *actus reus*, *mens rea*, circumstance elements, and criminal harm

F. Stalking—involves intentionally scaring another by conduct which falls short of assault and battery
   1. Anti-stalking statutes—tremendous variation among states
   2. Stalking *actus reus*
      a. All states require that the act be a repeated one.
      b. All states require some version of visual or physical proximity.
      c. About half the states include verbal or written threats, threats implied by conduct, threat, terrorist threat, or credible threat.
      d. Some states list very specific behavior.
   3. Stalking *mens rea*
      a. Specific intent to commit the forbidden *actus reus*.
      b. Some mental attitude (it varies) causing the bad result is also required.
      c. Just more than half the states require subjective fault.
      d. One-third of the states require objective fault.
   4. Bad result—placing the victim in fear
      a. Subjective and objective fear (most states and the model code)
      b. Subjective fear only test
      c. Objective fear only test
      d. Intent-to-instill-fear test
   5. Cyberstalking—using the internet to stalk another
      a. *Case: State v. Hoying*

IV. **Personal restraint crimes**: kidnapping and false imprisonment
   A. Laws protect the fundamental right of locomotion—the right to move about and come and go as we please.
   B. **Kidnapping**
      1. Elements of common-law kidnapping:
         a. Seizing, carrying away (asportation of), and confining another person
         b. By force or threat of force, fraud, or deception
         c. Intent to deprive the other person of her or his liberty
      2. Elements of modern kidnapping law
         a. ***Actus reus***—Asportation requirement recognizes even practically no movement of the victim.
            (1) *Case: People v. Chessman*
            (2) *Case: People v. Allen*
         b. ***Mens rea***—The specific intent to confine, significantly restrain, or hold victims in secret without the victim's consent.
      3. **Grading the seriousness** of kidnapping
         a. Simple
         b. Aggravated—aggravating circumstances include kidnapping for the purpose of:
            (1) Sexual invasion
            (2) Obtaining a hostage
            (3) Obtaining ransom
            (4) Robbing the victim
            (5) Murdering the victim

Study Guide

          (6) Blackmail
          (7) Terrorizing the victim
          (8) Achieving political aims

    C. **False imprisonment**
        1. *Actus reus*—keeping another person from moving freely (no asportation requirement)
        2. *Mens rea*—having the specific intent to confine or restrain another person without their consent

CHAPTER SUMMARY

Crimes against persons involve four types: taking a life (homicide), unwanted sexual invasions (rape and sex offenses), bodily injury (assault and battery), and personal restraint (kidnapping and false imprisonment). In one form or another, all of these were common-law crimes.

Sex offenses are serious even if there is no physical injury, because they violate intimacy, privacy, and bodily integrity in a way typical physical injuries cannot. The criminal justice system handles rapes by strangers and men with weapons well, but it doesn't do as well with the overwhelming number of rapes by men who know their victims, including date rape.

The old rape law defined a crime of forcible sexual penetration that only men could commit against women who weren't their wives. The elements of rape at common law were: 1) intentional vaginal intercourse; 2) between a man and a woman who was not his wife; 3) achieved by force or a threat of severe bodily harm; 4) without the woman's consent.

Modern statutes have expanded the crime of rape and other sex crimes in criminal sexual conduct statutes. These new offenses include a list of gender-neutral sex offenses, involving unwanted sexual penetrations and contacts. Rape in most jurisdictions today has four elements: 1) the *actus reus* of sexual penetration; 2) the *actus reus* of force, or threat of force, to accomplish sexual penetration (or some substitute such as unconsciousness, mental impairment, etc.); 3) the *mens rea* of intentional sexual penetration; and 4) the circumstance of the lack of victim consent.

One controversial issue is whether there should also be a specific intent element in rape. The leading case on the point is the controversial English case of *Regina v. Morgan* (1975). Morgan and three companions were drinking in a bar. When they failed to find female companionship, Morgan invited the others to come home with him to have sexual intercourse with his wife. Morgan told the others that she would want to have sex with them and would only pretend to resist. He told them not to worry if she struggled because she liked rough sex. The Sixth House of Lords (England's highest court) overturned the convictions because the defendants didn't specifically intend to have sexual intercourse without the victim's consent. Why? Because the defendants believed that Morgan's wife wanted sex and wanted the struggle.

When American courts face the intent question, they vary in their response. Many come down between the English specific-intent rule and strict liability on the issue of intent or knowledge to have sex without the victims consent. Some of these courts have adopted a reckless or negligent standard with regard to the consent problem.

Current rape law has shifted the emphasis from the resistance of victims to lack of consent. The traditional emphasis on physical violence (or threats thereof) to satisfy the element of force in the *actus reus* of rape is shifting in modern rape law to the sufficiency of non-consent to unwanted sexual activity.

According to the law, the prosecution has to prove non-consent by the victim beyond a reasonable doubt. However, as a matter of strategy, defendants claim victim consent as a defense.

Most current statutes divide rape into two degrees: simple (second-degree) rape and aggravated (first-degree) rape. Aggravated rape involves at least one of the following circumstances: victim suffers serious bodily injury, stranger rape, rape occurs in conjunction with another crime, rapist is armed, multiple offenders, or victim is a minor while the rapist is significantly older. All other rapes are "simple" rapes with lesser penalties.

Much of the law of rape and rape prosecutions has changed over the years. The marital exception and prompt report rule have been abolished in many jurisdictions. Corroboration of the victim's testimony is no longer required. Rape shield laws limit the ability of the defense to bring out evidence of the victim's prior sex life. Utmost resistance by the victim is no longer required. Reasonable resistance is enough.

Bodily injury crimes include unlawful nonsexual contacts (battery) or threats of them (assault). The elements of battery are negligently, recklessly, knowingly, or purposely causing and unlawful, offensive touching of another. The grading of the seriousness of a battery depends on the amount of injury and the circumstances of the touching.

An assault requires no touching. There are two kinds of assault: attempted battery (having the specific intent to commit battery and taking steps to complete it) and threatened battery (intentionally scaring the victim). In both types, the victim must be aware of the defendant's conduct.

Although stalking has occurred for centuries, in 1990, California enacted the first criminal stalking statute. Most states have since followed suit, but there is tremendous variation in these statutes. Stalking involves repeated, unwanted, and threatening conduct which either places the victim in fear or would cause a reasonable person to fear. Stalking is widespread and has major negative effects on its victims. Cyberstalking is a type of stalking in which the stalker uses the internet, e-mail, or electronic communication devices to threaten the victim.

Kidnapping and false imprisonment are crimes against the right to come and go as we please. At common law, kidnapping consisted of six elements: 1) seizing, 2) carrying away (asportation of) and 3) confining 4) another person 5) by force, threat of force, fraud, or deception 6) with the intent to deprive the other of their liberty.

The critical difference between false imprisonment and kidnapping is that the *actus reus* of asportation (carrying away) of victims is required in kidnapping. Modern interpretations have rendered the asportation requirement of kidnapping almost meaningless.

Kidnapping is usually divided into two degrees: simple and aggravated. The most common aggravating circumstances include kidnapping for the purpose of sexual invasion, taking a hostage, getting ransom, terrorizing the victim, and achieving political goals. The penalty for aggravated kidnapping is typically life imprisonment and, until recently, even death.

The elements of false imprisonment are restraining another person's liberty, with specific intent to restrain. The Model Penal Code requires the restraint to "interfere substantially with the victim's liberty," but in most states, any interference with another person's liberty suffices. In many states, false imprisonment means forcibly, by threat, or secretly confining, abducting, imprisoning, or restraining another person against their will and without legal authority.

Chapter 10: Crimes Against Persons II: Criminal Sexual Conduct—Bodily Injury, and Personal Restraint

PRACTICE TEST BANK

MULTIPLE CHOICE

1. Asportation is an element of kidnapping. Asportation refers to _____.

    a. confining
    b. alleviating
    c. carrying away
    d. restraining

2. The crime of kidnapping has _____ *mens rea* element(s).

    a. no
    b. one
    c. two
    d. three

3. False imprisonment and kidnapping are _____ crimes.

    a. specific-intent
    b. strict liability
    c. *mala prohibita*
    d. inchoate

4. The *actus reus* of false imprisonment is _____.

    a. carrying away
    b. threats
    c. abducting
    d. restraint

5. One difference between false imprisonment and kidnapping is that false imprisonment _____.

    a. is a felony
    b. is a strict liability crime
    c. has no asportation element
    d. has only one *actus reus*

6. Prior to recent reforms, proof of lack of consent in rape prosecutions _____.

    a. was irrelevant to the crime of rape
    b. could be established by verbal resistance alone
    c. required proof of physical resistance
    d. required that the defendant show physical signs of being forcibly resisted

7. A battery is an unlawful _____.

    a. attempted assault
    b. felony
    c. aggravated assault
    d. offensive touching of another

8. Modern assault and/or battery statutes often _____.

    a. have made them capital offenses
    b. have negligence and recklessness as a *mens rea*
    c. have made them strict liability crimes
    d. have eliminated purposeful as a *mens rea*

9. The extrinsic force standard of rape requires that the rapist have used _____.

    a. only the force necessary to accomplish the penetration itself
    b. force beyond that necessary to penetrate the victim
    c. only a reasonable amount of force to accomplish the penetration itself
    d. only reasonable force to overcome the victim's resistance

10. In *Regina v. Morgan*, Britain's highest court held that the defendants were not guilty of rape because _____.

    a. they reasonably believed the victim was old enough to give valid consent
    b. did not use force on the victim
    c. they reasonably believe the victim consented
    d. the statute had no specific intent requirement

11. In statutory rape cases, the rule in most states is that _____.

    a. there is a defense that the victim was promiscuous
    b. a reasonable mistake as to consent is a defense
    c. there is no *mens rea* in the crime
    d. there is no mistake of age defense

Chapter 10: Crimes Against Persons II: Criminal Sexual Conduct—Bodily Injury, and Personal Restraint

12. Under the common law, _____.

    a. there were only two sex crimes—rape and sodomy
    b. there were no sex crimes
    c. rape was the only sex crime
    d. sodomy was the only sex crime

13. In the 1950s, courts began to relax the traditional _____ victim resistance standard and replaced it with a reasonable resistance standard for rape victims.

    a. maximum
    b. utmost
    c. contingent
    d. foreseeable

14. Rape shield statutes _____.

    a. limit evidence of the victim's reputation or past sexual conduct
    b. shield the victim from the media
    c. prohibit cross examination of the rape victim
    d. protect the defendant from prejudicial pretrial publicity

15. In many jurisdictions today, rape statutes have modified the common law by _____.

    a. excluding any defense of victim consent
    b. making rape a capital felony
    c. making the offense gender neutral
    d. eliminating the martial exception

16. Many states now have an offense called felonious or _____ assault which is an assault plus other elements such as causing serious bodily injury, using a deadly weapon, or assaulting a peace officer.

    a. grand
    b. aggravated
    c. mitigated
    d. serious

17. The Model Penal Code is different from both the common law and many state statutes in that the Model Penal Code definition of simple assault _____.

    a. has no offensive touching *actus reus*
    b. provides that assault can be committed vicariously
    c. makes assault a strict liability crime
    d. has no *actus reus* element

18. The offense of _____ rape involves an adult having sex with a child, even if the child consents.

    a. child indecency
    b. criminal contact
    c. statutory
    d. minority

19. Traditionally, all assaults were _____.

    a. felonies
    b. *mala prohibita*
    c. misdemeanors
    d. strict liability crimes

20. In common-law rape trials, the victims must have _____ in order to get a conviction.

    a. reported the rape promptly
    b. been unmarried
    c. been over the age of fourteen
    d. been under the age of twelve

21. The crime of rape generally _____.

    a. requires that actual extrinsic force be used against the victim
    b. includes threats of imminent force
    c. has no circumstance element
    d. has no *actus reus* element

22. In many modern rape, sexual assault, and criminal sexual conduct statutes, such as that in Minnesota, _____.

    a. a female could be guilty of a penetration crime
    b. the marital exception is retained
    c. the corroboration requirement is retained
    d. have only one degree of offense

23. In most statutes today, _____.

    a. the formerly separate offenses of assault and battery are combined
    b. all assaults are felonies
    c. all batteries are misdemeanors
    d. the common-law offenses of battery and aggravated assault are combined

24. Offensive physical contact of another is _____.

    a. always criminal
    b. the *actus reus* of battery
    c. the *actus reus* of assault
    d. the *mens rea* of mayhem

25. Intentionally spitting in someone's face to insult them _____.

    a. cannot be a crime
    b. could be an assault
    c. can be a battery
    d. can be an aggravated assault

26. If a person's dog attacks and injures a victim, the person _____.

    a. cannot be guilty of any crime unless the person intended that the victim be injured
    b. can only be sued civilly by the victim. There is no crime.
    c. is guilty of battery only if the victim provoked the animal
    d. can be guilty of an assault or battery

27. Intentionally and repeatedly following a person to scare or harass them is usually referred to as the crime of _____.

    a. intimidation
    b. stalking
    c. terroristic threats
    d. habitual harassment

28. The societal value offended by kidnapping and false imprisonment is personal _____.

    a. privacy
    b. solitude
    c. liberty
    d. integrity

29. Kidnapping can be committed by force, threat of force, and _____.

    a. confounding or compounding
    b. mendacity or veracity
    c. fraud or deception
    d. culpability and mendacity

Study Guide

30. Perhaps the most famous kidnapping case of the 1970s involved the kidnapping of heiress _____.

    a. Paula Lindbergh
    b. Pat Hauptman
    c. Patricia Hearst
    d. Priscilla Lowry

TRUE/FALSE

1. In the Model Penal Code, and most states, simple assault is a felony.
    a. true
    b. false

2. Cyberstalking constitutes approximately 50 percent of all stalking.
    a. true
    b. false

3. The crimes of kidnapping and false imprisonment are specific-intent crimes.
    a. true
    b. false

4. Certain types of motives can turn a simple kidnapping into an aggravated kidnapping.
    a. true
    b. false

5. False imprisonment always requires actual use of force.
    a. true
    b. false

6. Modern interpretations of the asportation element of kidnapping require only slight movement of the victim or render it virtually meaningless.
    a. true
    b. false

7. At common law, the offense of kidnapping had only three elements.
    a. true
    b. false

8. At common law, a man could not be guilty of raping his wife.
    a. true
    b. false

9. Rape law reform began seriously in the 1920s.
   a. true
   b. false

10. In some jurisdictions, an aggravated rape is one where the rapist is armed or the victim suffers serious bodily injury.
    a. true
    b. false

11. The *actus reus* of assault is offensive touching.
    a. true
    b. false

12. False imprisonment is a vicarious liability crime.
    a. true
    b. false

13. The most famous kidnapping case of the 1970s was the kidnapping and murder of Charles Lindbergh's infant son.
    a. true
    b. false

14. One difference between false imprisonment and kidnapping is that only kidnapping requires asportation of the victim.
    a. true
    b. false

15. At common law, the crime of rape was punishable by death.
    a. true
    b. false

16. At common law, rape was a specific-intent crime.
    a. true
    b. false

17. If the rape victim is mentally deficient, incapacitated by alcohol or drugs, or otherwise not capable of giving a valid consent, it can still be rape even though no force was used or threatened.
    a. true
    b. false

18. Beginning in the 1990s, most states began repealing their rape shield laws.
    a. true
    b. false

19. Over time, the reasonable resistance standard came to be replaced by an utmost resistance standard.
    a. true
    b. false

20. Stalking is a relatively recent phenomenon.
    a. true
    b. false

21. In most modern rape laws, lack of consent of the victim is not a circumstance element.
    a. true
    b. false

22. The extrinsic force standard requires more force than the intrinsic force standard.
    a. true
    b. false

23. Only a few states allow the defense of reasonable mistake of age in statutory rape cases.
    a. true
    b. false

24. Victim consent is a defense to statutory rape.
    a. true
    b. false

25. In a statutory rape case, the prosecution must prove some force or threat of force by the defendant to convict.
    a. true
    b. false

FILL-IN-THE-BLANK

1. The term _____ means carrying away.

2. _____ rape involves sex with a young person, even without force.

3. The only two common-law sex offenses were rape and _____.

4. The circumstance element of most modern rape laws is _____ of the victim.

5. The *actus reus* of rape is sexual _____ of the victim.

6. In some states, a reasonable mistake of fact with regard to the victim's _____ is a defense to statutory rape.

7. Intentionally restraining someone's liberty is the offense of _____ imprisonment.

8. The *actus reus* of traditional assault is a/n _____ or threatened battery.

9. Rape _____ laws limit evidence about a rape victim's past and reputation.

10. The _____ standard requires more force than just the force needed to penetrate the victim.

11. Most sex crime statutes today are _____ neutral.

12. If mistake as to the victim's age is a defense to rape, the mistake or belief must be _____.

13. In general, assaults or batteries that cause _____ bodily injury are felonies.

14. _____ threats cannot be an assault, because the threat of harm is not immediate.

15. The _____ force standard requires only the force necessary to cause penetration of the victim.

Study Guide

ESSAY

1. Discuss the various approaches taken to combat stalking and the harm caused by it.

2. Over time, how has the law of rape changed with regard to force and consent?

3. Compare and contrast the crimes (and elements) of kidnapping and false imprisonment.

4. Compare and contrast the crimes of assault and battery.

5. Compare and contrast the elements of rape at common law with the typical rape statute today.

Chapter 10: Crimes Against Persons II: Criminal Sexual Conduct—Bodily Injury, and Personal Restraint

CHAPTER 10 ANSWER KEY

Multiple Choice

1. c	2. b	3. a	4. d	5. c
6. c	7. d	8. b	9. b	10. c
11. d	12. a	13. b	14. a	15. d
16. b	17. a	18. c	19. c	20. a
21. b	22. a	23. a	24. b	25. b
26. d	27. b	28. c	29. c	30. c

True/False

1. F	2. F	3. T	4. T	5. F
6. T	7. F	8. T	9. F	10. T
11. F	12. F	13. F	14. T	15. T
16. F	17. T	18. F	19. F	20. F
21. F	22. T	23. T	24. F	25. F

Fill-in-the-Blank

1. asportation	2. Statutory	3. sodomy
4. non-consent	5. penetration	6. age
7. false	8. attempted	9. shield
10. extrinsic force	11. gender	12. reasonable
13. serious	14. Conditional	15. intrinsic

CHAPTER 11
CRIMES AGAINST PROPERTY

LEARNING OBJECTIVES

After studying this chapter, students will understand that:

- Crimes against other people's property are of three types: taking property, damaging or destroying property, and invading property.

- The crime of theft grew out of the general social concern with violent crimes against persons.

- It's illegal to receive stolen property only if you intend to keep it permanently.

- The heart of robbery is the use of actual or threatened force to obtain someone else's property right now.

- Extortion differs from robbery in that the threat is to use force some time in the future.

- Arson is a felony; criminal mischief is a misdemeanor.

- The heart of both burglary and criminal trespass is *invading* other people's property, not taking, destroying, or damaging it.

- Criminal trespass used to be limited to unauthorized invasions of physical property, but now it includes unauthorized access to electronic information systems.

- Identity theft is the most prevalent crime in the United States.

- Intellectual property theft results in billions of dollars in losses each year.

KEY TERMS AND CONCEPTS

- **cybercrimes**—crimes committed through the internet or some other computer network; p. 370

- **robbery**—taking and carrying away another's property by force or threat of force with the intent to permanently deprive the owner of possession; p. 371

- **larceny**—taking and carrying away another person's property without the use of force with the intent to permanently deprive its owner of possession; p. 371

Chapter 11: Crimes Against Property

- **tangible property**—personal property (not real estate); p. 371
- **intangible property**—property that lacks a physical existence (examples include stock options, trademarks, licenses, and patents); p. 371
- **embezzlement**—the crime of lawfully gaining possession of someone else's property and later converting it to one's own use; p. 371
- **abuse-of-trust crimes (in property crime)**—crimes committed by caretakers; p. 371
- **white-collar crimes**—crimes growing out of opportunities to get someone else's property provided by the perpetrator's occupation; p. 371
- **false pretenses**—in modern law, it's often called "theft by deceit," and it means having the specific intent to obtain property by deceit and lies; p. 372
- **theft by deceit or trick**—obtaining someone else's property by deceit and lies; p. 372
- **theft**—the consolidated crimes of larceny, embezzlement, and false pretenses; p. 372
- **consolidated theft statutes**—eliminate the artificial need to separate theft into distinct offenses according to their *actus reus*; p. 372
- **receiving stolen property**—benefiting from someone else's property without having participated in the wrongful acquisition in the first place; p. 373
- **extortion (blackmail)**—misappropriation of another's property by means of threats to inflict bodily harm in the future; p. 381
- **arson**—intentionally burning a house or other structure; p. 381
- **criminal mischief (in property crimes)**—misdemeanor of damaging or destroying other people's property; p. 381
- **burning (*actus reus* in arson)**—setting a building on fire, and the fire actually reaches the structure; p. 382
- **burglary**—breaking and entering a building with intent to commit a crime inside the building; p. 387
- **criminal trespass (in property crimes)**—the crime of invading another person's property; p. 387

- **surreptitious remaining element**—entering a structure lawfully with the intent to commit a crime inside; p. 389

- **intellectual property**—information and services stored in and transmitted to and from electronic data banks; a rapidly developing area of property crimes; p. 393

- **identity theft**—stealing another person's identity for the purpose of getting something of value; p. 393

CHAPTER OUTLINE

I. Taking other people's property
    A. History of property crimes
        1. General concern about violent crimes led to crime of common-law robbery.
            a. Taking someone else's property by force
        2. Larceny
            a. Taking and carrying away
            b. Intent to permanently deprive someone else of their property
            c. Tangible personal property (property valuable itself, like a ring)
            d. Intangible personal property (paper that represents something of value like stocks, bonds, checks)
        3. Embezzlement (first white-collar crime)
            a. Keeping (converting) property lawfully obtained
            b. "Converting" substitutes for "taking" in larceny
            c. Caretakers (bailees) taking someone else's property that was handed over to them voluntarily (like bank clerks).
                (1) Abuse-of-trust crimes
                (2) White-collar crimes
        4. False pretenses (theft by deceit)
            a. Tricking (deceiving) someone into giving up their property
            b. Deceiving substitutes for taking in larceny and converting in embezzlements.
    B. **Theft**
        1. Modern consolidated theft statutes—turn away from history to logic in consolidating embezzlement larceny, and false pretenses into one crime of theft: getting other people's money by taking, converting, or deceiving
        2. Elements
            a. Purposefully (intentionally), or knowingly
            b. Taking and carrying away, converting, or swindling
            c. Someone else's property

C. **Receiving Stolen Property**
 1. It is a crime not only to take someone else's property but also to "receive" (accept) property already stolen.
 2. *Actus reus*—receiving means controlling (not necessarily physically) property.
 3. *Mens rea* varies from knowingly to recklessly to negligently, depending on the state.
 4. *Mens rea* also includes the intent to keep the property permanently.
    a. *Case: Sonnier v. State*
    b. *Case: In the Interest of C.W.*
D. **Robbery**—Crimes against persons and property
 1. **Robbery** *actus reus*—taking and carrying away someone else's property by force or threat of immediate force
    a. *Case: State v. Curley*
    b. *Case: Commonwealth v. Zangari*
 2. **Robbery** *mens rea*—intent to take property from another person by force or threat of immediate force
 3. **Degrees of Robbery**—measured by
    a. Force (kind and degree) used
    b. Injury (kind and degree) inflicted
E. **Extortion** (blackmail)
 1. Circumstance of time distinguishes extortion from robbery
 2. Extortion elements
    a. *Actus reus*—taking someone else's property by threat of a variety of future harms
    b. *Mens rea*—intent to take someone else's property by threat of future harm

II. Damaging and destroying other people's property
A. Arson
 1. **Arson** *actus reus*: **burning**
    a. *Case: Williams v. State*
 2. **Arson** *mens rea*—intent to commit the act of burning or setting fire to a building (not necessary to intend to damage or destroy the building)
 3. **The degrees of arson**
    a. First degree—burning occupied buildings
    b. Second degree—burning unoccupied structures
B. **Criminal Mischief**
 1. **Criminal mischief** *actus reus*—burning, exploding, flooding, or committing some other dangerous act; could include tampering (creating danger to property)
 2. **Criminal mischief** *mens rea*—varies tremendously amongst states
    a. *Case: Commonwealth v. Mitchell*

III. Invading other people's property
   A. **Burglary**
      1. **Common law burglary elements**
         a. Breaking and entering; of dwelling place of another; at night; with intent to commit a felony therein.
      2. **Burglary *actus reus***—entering or remaining in (and in a few states "breaking into") someone else's "structure"
         a. **Circumstances**—Is the structure occupied? Is it another's place? Is it nighttime?
         b. *Case: Jewell v. State*
      3. **Burglary *mens rea***—specific-intent crime
         a. Intent to commit the breaking, entering, or remaining
         b. Intent to commit a crime once inside the structure
      4. **Degrees of burglary**
         a. According to seriousness
         b. According to the type of structure
   B. **Criminal Trespass**—heart of crime is unwanted presence
      1. **The elements of criminal trespass**
         a. Unauthorized entering or remaining on the premises of another
      2. **The degrees of criminal trespass**
         a. MPC has three: misdemeanor, petty misdemeanor, and violation
   C. **Cybercrimes**
      1. **Identity theft**
         a. Currently one of the most prevalent crimes—taking someone else's property by first stealing their identity.
         b. Huge consequences, but difficult to catch
         c. Family members, friends, and neighbors get information from credit cards, utility services, bank accounts, etc.
         d. *Case: Remsburg v. Docusearch, Inc.*
      2. **Intellectual Property Theft**
         a. Taking people's ideas
         b. Protected by copyright laws, laws on trademarks, trade secrets, patents, theft, damage, and destruction of intellectual property
         c. Hackers and cybercriminals
         a. *Case: U. S. v. Ancheta*

CHAPTER SUMMARY

Crimes against property are one of three types: taking it, damaging or destroying it, or invading it. In recent centuries, technology has afforded many new ways to steal. The new crimes created to deal with the new types of property crime are really only new ways of committing the three original types of crimes. Computer and internet crimes consist of taking, damaging or destroying, or invading other people's computers or the information stored on them.

Historically, all crimes of taking property descend from larceny, which means sneaking away with (stealing) someone else's property. However, as times changed, other crimes developed to address the fact that sometimes people wrongfully take property entrusted to them (embezzlement) or trick people into obtaining title of the property (false pretenses). Modern consolidated theft statutes now deal with the various ways people acquire other's property (sneaking away, converting, through fraud). Theft (or larceny) is a specific-intent crime; it requires the intent to permanently deprive the other person of their property.

Obtaining property already stolen by someone else still is regarded as a crime. Traditionally, it was called receiving stolen property.

Robbery is a crime against persons and their property. It involves taking someone else's property from their person by force or the threat of immediate force. Robbery consists of three elements. The *actus reus* components are: 1) the taking and carrying away, 2) by immediate force or the threat of immediate force, 3) another person's property from their body or presence. The *mens rea* is the intent to permanently deprive the victim of their property by immediate force or the threat of immediate force. The circumstance element is that the property is taken from the victim's person or presence.

Extortion (also called blackmail) is a crime against persons and their property. Theft by extortion is taking someone else's property by threats of future harm. Time separates extortion from robbery—robbery is a threat to hurt someone right now if they don't give up their property; and extortion is a threat to hurt someone later. The elements of extortion consist of *mens rea*—the specific intent to take someone else's property by means of threats; and *actus reus*—a specific threat by which the taking of property is accomplished.

Arson (damaging or destroying other people's buildings by fire or explosives) is a felony. Criminal mischief (destroying or tampering with other people's property or causing money loss by "expensive practical jokes" or false threats) is a misdemeanor. Criminal mischief includes three types of harm to tangible property: 1) destruction or damage by fire, explosives, or other "dangerous acts" (the original malicious mischief); 2) tampering with tangible property so as to endanger it; and 3) deception or threat that causes monetary loss.

The elements of common-law burglary from which our modern burglary emerged included: 1) breaking and entering (*actus reus*), 2) the dwelling of another (circumstance element), 3) in the nighttime (circumstance element), 4) with the intent to commit a felony inside (*mens rea*). Modern burglary has outgrown its common-law origin of just protecting homes. Now, you can "burglarize" all kinds of structures, even vehicles, at any time of the day. The breaking and entering elements have been eliminated or modified, and the predicate crimes do not always have to be a felony.

A less serious crime related to burglary is criminal trespass. The *actus reus* of criminal trespass is the unauthorized entering of or remaining on the premises of another. The *mens rea* varies, including 1) knowingly enters or remains without authority invitation, license privilege, or legality; 2) specific intent to enter or remain without authority for some unlawful purpose (a few states); or 3) strict liability.

Although relatively new, cybercrime is the most common crime in America. It consists of identity theft and intellectual property theft. Identity theft involves taking another's property by stealing their name and personal information (their identity). Intellectual property theft is taking someone's ideas or creative endeavors. Cybercrime involves the use of computers to gain access to identity, ideas, or creative endeavors. Cybercriminals are smart, skilled, and motivated; and catching intellectual property and identity thieves is very difficult.

PRACTICE TEST BANK

MULTIPLE CHOICE

1. A person who receives stolen property and then resells it is called a _____.

    a. unlawful receiver
    b. unlawful wholesaler
    c. larceny receptor
    d. fence

2. At common law, the offense of burglary _____.

    a. could only be committed at night
    b. included all types of buildings
    c. required entering but not breaking
    d. was a strict liability crime

3. Under modern approaches to burglary and assuming all the elements, if the burglar entered the building unlawfully, in an unusual fashion, such as coming down the chimney, this _____.

    a. could not be a burglary because there was no breaking
    b. could be a burglary but only if the building was occupied
    c. could still be a burglarly
    d. is not a burglary because there was no unlawful entry

4. In many states, and the Model Penal Code, the *actus reus* of arson requires _____.

    a. only that the defendant start a fire
    b. that some part of the building be charred
    c. that some damage to the building occur
    d. that some part of the building be burned

5. At common law, the intent to commit a crime in the dwelling required that the intended crime be _____.

    a. a crime of violence
    b. a felony
    c. any form of theft
    d. any property crime

6. In contrast to earlier law burglary law, by 1900 in most statutes _____.

    a. the breaking element became a mere technicality
    b. the breaking element evolved into a strict liability offense
    c. the requirement of intent to commit a crime in the building was eliminated
    d. the requirement that the building be occupied at the time of the burglary was eliminated

7. In addition to the unlawful entry version of burglary, the Model Penal Code and some jurisdictions also have a/n _____ version of burglary.

    a. surreptitious remaining
    b. constructive concealment
    c. constructive burglary
    d. entry by deceit

8. In the case of *U.S. v. Ancheta*, the defendant unlawfully got rich by _____.

    a. stealing someone's identity
    b. planting a worm in computers used by the federal government to commit fraud
    c. receiving stolen property from the largest heist in America
    d. engaging in salami attacks and siphoning off small amounts of money from millions of accounts

9. In *Remsburg v. Docusearch*, the information given to Youens enabled him to _____.

    a. use the victim's identity to purchase airline tickets
    b. plant a worm in a computer
    c. obtain a social security number and get gainful employment
    d. find and kill someone

10. Most states have attempted to better organize theft law by enacting _____ statutes.

    a. omnibus larceny
    b. comprehensive larceny
    c. complete theft
    d. consolidated theft

11. The specific-intent element of receiving stolen property is _____.

    a. knowing the property is stolen
    b. receiving property
    c. deceiving the true owner
    d. finding property that is stolen

12. A trademark is a type of _____.

    a. tangible property
    b. intellectual property
    c. identity property
    d. personal property

13. Criminal trespass can be accomplished through entry _____.

    a. onto land only
    b. onto land and into buildings
    c. onto land, into buildings, and through computers
    d. into buildings only

14. The court in *Jewell v. State* found that Jewell could be liable for burglary because _____.

    a. the court found that the house had never been his because Bridget had bought it in her name
    b. the court found that the statute's requirement "of another" was satisfied by unauthorized entry
    c. the court found that Jewell and the victim were divorced
    d. Jewell obviously had the intent to commit assault when he entered through the kitchen window

15. Which of the following is NOT a reason for the nighttime requirement of common-law burglary?

    a. It was easier to commit crimes at night.
    b. It is harder to identify suspects you've seen at night.
    c. Nighttime intrusions frighten victims more than daytime intrusions.
    d. At common law, there were no police officers at night.

16. A _____ is a person who has the stolen property between the thief and a purchaser.

    a. fence
    b. purveyor
    c. procurer
    d. provocateur

17. The offense of burglary has _____ *mens rea* elements.

    a. two
    b. three
    c. four
    d. five

18. Which of the following elements of common-law burglary is retained in most modern statutes?

    a. The burglary occurred at night.
    b. The entry must be unlawful.
    c. The building must be a dwelling.
    d. There must be an actual, physical breaking.

19. Under modern statutes, the crime the burglar intended to commit inside the building _____.

    a. must be a crime that is *mala prohibita*
    b. has been expanded beyond the common-law rule of felonies only
    c. is limited to crimes of theft
    d. must be a felony as also required at common law

20. If a person is apprehended while unlawfully on someone else's property, but there is no evidence of another crime, or intent to commit another crime, the proper charge would be _____.

    a. burglary
    b. criminal trespass
    c. attempted invasion of privacy
    d. discrepancy

21. The offense of burglary is a crime that has _____.

    a. no *mens rea* elements
    b. a general-intent component but not a specific-intent element
    c. a specific-intent, but not a general-intent
    d. both specific- and general-intent elements

22. The specific-intent of robbery is intent to _____.

    a. harm the victim
    b. permanently deprive the victim of the property
    c. commit a crime
    d. obtain title to the property

23. One of the circumstance elements of burglary is _____.

    a. type of structure
    b. constructive breaking
    c. intent to enter unlawfully
    d. surreptitious remaining

24. Which of the following are *mens rea* elements of burglary?

    a   intent to damage or destroy the building
    b   intent to break and enter or surreptitiously remain
    c   intent to deprive the owner of possession and ownership of the structure
    d. intent to surprise and harm the persons in the structure

25. As compared to burglary, criminal trespass has _____.

    a. fewer elements
    b. greater penalties
    c. more elements
    d. a longer history

26. The *mens rea* in most types of arson is intent to _____.

    a. destroy a building by fire
    b. enter a building to start a fire
    c. set a fire to a building
    d. break into a building and start a fire

27. The defendant walks into the bank while it is open to the public and hides in the public restroom. After the bank closes he attempts break into the vault. This is the _____ type of burglary.

    a. privileged entry
    b. surreptitious remaining
    c. false pretenses
    d. constructive entry

28. Many incidents that were burglaries at common law would today _____.

    a. be criminal trespasses
    b. not be crimes
    c. be *mala in se* crimes
    d. also be burglaries

29. The law of criminal trespass has been expanded beyond its traditional coverage to now include _____ trespass.

    a. real estate
    b. personal property
    c. computer
    d. curtilage

Study Guide

30. The practice of employees and insiders altering or manipulating data, credit limits, or other financial information is called _____.

    a. piggybacking
    b. sniffing
    c. data diddling
    d. a salami attack

TRUE/FALSE

1. At common law, walking through a wide open door into a home to commit a felony therein was a burglary.
    a. true
    b. false

2. To be guilty of burglary, the burglar does not have to complete the crime he intended to commit.
    a. true
    b. false

3. The modern definition of burglary is narrower than the common-law definition.
    a. true
    b. false

4. The two offenses that involve both thefts and force or threat of force are robbery and burglary.
    a. true
    b. false

5. Picking a pocket without any additional action or force by the defendant is not a robbery.
    a. true
    b. false

6. In some states, a purse snatching, where the victim is not threatened and does not resist, and the purse is not otherwise attached to the person, is not a robbery.
    a. true
    b. false

7. Intellectual property theft requires the use of computers.
    a. true
    b. false

8. Robbery requires that the robber threaten to use force immediately.
   a. true
   b. false

9. The *mens rea* of extortion is the specific intent to obtain property by deceit.
   a. true
   b. false

10. The definition of arson has contracted as compared to its definition at common law.
    a. true
    b. false

11. Most arson statutes create specific-intent crimes.
    a. true
    b. false

12. The *actus reus* of arson is to set fire to a structure.
    a. true
    b. false

13. Extortion is a strict liability crime.
    a. true
    b. false

14. Many states divide arson into one or more degrees or types.
    a. true
    b. false

15. Surreptitious remaining is a type of extortion.
    a. true
    b. false

16. Abuse-of-trust crimes, such as embezzlement, eventually became white-collar crimes.
    a. true
    b. false

17. For common-law burglary, a *mens rea* element was that the crime occurred at night.
    a. true
    b. false

18. Until the 1900s, the *actus reus* of burglary consisted of only constructive breaking.
    a. true
    b. false

19. At common law, the breaking element of burglary was by a surreptitious remaining element.
    a. true
    b. false

20. Robbery is a crime against both persons and property.
    a. true
    b. false

21. Robbery has a specific-intent element.
    a. true
    b. false

22. Robbery has a circumstance element.
    a. true
    b. false

23. While picking a pocket, the thief is grabbed by the victim. The thief pushes the victim away and takes the wallet. This is a robbery.
    a. true
    b. false

24. Most robbery victims are physically harmed.
    a. true
    b. false

25. Identity theft involves the violation of copyright and trademark laws.
    a. true
    b. false

FILL-IN-THE-BLANK

1. The common law *mens rea* of arson was that it be done willfully and _____.

2. Some states have removed the unlawful _____ element to create a new form of burglary by surreptitious remaining.

3. The Model Penal Code limits the crime of burglary to _____ structures or vehicles.

4. The _____ crime is the crime the burglar intends to commit inside the building.

5. The illegal use or keeping of someone else's property is called _____.

6. The form of theft involving lies or deception is called _____.

7. Robbery involves taking property from the victim's person or _____.

8. A _____ is a series of minor computer crimes (such as hacking into a computer and taking one penny from each account) which is difficult to detect.

9. The *actus reus* of common-law burglary is breaking and _____.

10. Many states have combined a number of types of theft into one statute that is termed a _____ theft statute.

11. Personal property, which can be physically held, is called _____.

12. _____ is the unlawful entry or remaining on property or in a building of another.

13. If a pickpocket must push or shove the victim to get the wallet, the crime becomes one of _____.

14. _____ is permanently keeping someone's property when you only have a temporary right to possess it.

15. Trade secrets, information, programs, and data are known as _____ property.

ESSAY

1. Compare and contrast intellectual property crimes and identity theft crimes. How has the rise of computer use enhanced these crimes?

2. Trace the development of the law of theft and related offenses from common law to modern codes.

3. Trace the development of the law of burglary from common law to modern codes.

4. Compare and contrast robbery and extortion.

5. Compare and contrast arson, burglary, and criminal trespass.

CHAPTER 11 ANSWER KEY

Multiple Choice

1. d   2. a   3. c   4. a   5. b

6. a   7. a   8. b   9. d   10. d

11. a   12. b   13. c   14. b   15. d

16. a   17. a   18. b   19. b   20. b

21. d   22. b   23. a   24. b   25. a

26. c   27. b   28. d   29. c   30. c

True/False

1. F   2. T   3. F   4. F   5. T

6. T   7. F   8. T   9. F   10. F

11. F   12. T   13. F   14. T   15. F

16. T   17. F   18. F   19. F   20. T

21. T   22. T   23. T   24. F   25. F

Fill-in-the-Blank

1. maliciously   2. entry   3. occupied

4. predicate   5. conversion   6. false pretenses

7. presence   8. salami attack   9. entering

10. consolidated   11. tangible property   12. Criminal trespass

13. robbery   14. Embezzlement   15. intellectual

CHAPTER 12
CRIMES AGAINST PUBLIC ORDER AND MORALS

LEARNING OBJECTIVES

After studying this chapter, students will understand that:

- Some disorderly conduct crimes are now called "quality of life" crimes, but they're still aimed at the same conduct—"bad manners" in public.

- Efforts to control bad manners in public underscore the tension between order and liberty in constitutional democracies.

- Quality-of-life crimes are minor offenses, but the "broken windows" theory claims (based on mixed empirical results) they're linked to serious crime.

- There's widespread public support among all classes, races, and communities for controlling the bad behaviors of "street people" and "street gangs."

- Most people are more worried about bad public manners than they are about serious crimes.

- "Victimless" crimes against public decency (the ancient "crimes against public morals") are a hot-button issue between those who believe the criminal law should enforce morality and those who believe the nonviolent behavior of competent adults is none of the law's business.

KEY TERMS AND CONCEPTS

- **quality-of-life crimes**—breaches of minimum standards of decent behavior in public; p. 408

- **order**—behavior in public that comports with minimum community standards of civility; p. 408

- **liberty**—the right of individuals to go about in public, free of undue interference; p. 408

- **crimes against public order**—crimes that harm the public peace generally (for example, disorderly conduct); p. 408

- **"victimless" crimes**—crimes without complaining victims (for example, recreational illegal drug users); p. 408

Chapter 12: Crimes Against Public Order and Morals

- **disorderly conduct**—crimes against public order and morals; p. 409

- **actual disorderly conduct**—completed disorderly conduct (fighting); p. 409

- **constructive disorderly conduct**—acts that tend toward causing others to breach the peace; p. 409

- **unlawful assembly**—ancient crime of three or more persons gathering together to commit an unlawful act; p. 411

- **rout**—three or more people moving toward the commission of a riot; p. 411

- **riot**—disorderly conduct committed by more than three persons; p. 411

- **broken-windows theory**—theory that minor offenses or disorderly conduct can lead to a rise in serious crime; p. 412

- **vagrancy**—ancient crime of poor people wandering around with no visible means of support; p. 413

- **loitering**—remaining in one place with no apparent purpose; p. 413

- **preliminary injunction**—a temporary order issued by a court after giving notice and holding a hearing; p. 415

- **panhandling**—stopping people on the street to ask them for food or money; p. 418

- **time, place, and manner test**—three-part test to determine whether a statute places legitimate limits on the First Amendment right of free speech; p. 419

- **injunction to abate public nuisances**—an action in which city attorneys ask the courts to declare gang activities and gang members public nuisances and to issue injunctions to abate their activities; p. 422

CHAPTER OUTLINE

I. Disorderly conduct crimes can involved group or individual activity.
  A. Historically, these were largely ignored misdemeanors.
  B. Purposes for Model Penal Code provision
    1. Define *actus reus* more precisely than "disorderly conduct"
    2. Add a *mens rea* element to what used to be strict liability offenses
  C. **Individual disorderly conduct** in Model Penal Code
    1. *Actus reus*—three kinds
      a. Fighting
      b. Making unreasonable noise, using offensive language
      c. Creating hazardous or offensive conditions
    2. *Mens rea*—acting purposely, knowingly, or recklessly
    3. Special individual disorderly conduct sections in Model Penal Code
      a. Knowingly spreading false alarms
      b. Appearing drunk in public (no *mens rea* requirement)
      c. Loitering or prowling (no *mens rea* requirement)
      d. Purposely or recklessly obstructing highways or other public passages
      e. Purposely disrupting lawful meetings, processions, or gatherings
  D. **Group disorderly conduct** ("riot")
    1. Background
      a. Three ancient misdemeanor crimes (unlawful assembly, rout, riot)
      b. Riot Act of 1714—made riot a felony
      c. "Reading the riot act" comes from this act
    2. Elements
      a. *Actus reus*—participate in disorderly conduct
      b. *Mens rea*
        (1) Have specific intent or purpose to commit or facilitate the commission of a felony
        (2) Have the purpose to prevent or coerce an official action
        (3) Have knowledge that any participant used or plans to use a deadly weapon

II. Quality-of-life crimes involved both constitutional and criminological concerns.
  A. These crimes attempt to control "bad manners" in public places (sidewalks, streets, parks).
  B. Ancient offenses (crimes against public order) applied to new situations ("street people" and "gangs") called by a new name ("quality-of-life crimes").
  C. They underscore the tension between liberty and order in a constitutional democracy.
  D. Are the application of due process of liberty (Chapter 2) to maintaining order in public
  E. Broken-windows theory
    1. Theory—There's a link between "minor" quality-of-life offenses (public drunkenness, panhandling, graffiti, vandalism, prostitution, loitering) and serious crimes (rape, robbery, burglary).

2. Reality
    a. National debate concentrates on serious crime; local officials and public more worried about quality-of-life offenses.
    b. Empirical findings mixed as to link between serious crime and disorder.
        (1) Some find a causal relationship (Kelling, Skogan).
        (2) Others find common origins but not a causal link (Sampson and Radenbush).
F. Wide public agreement on what "bad public manners" consists of
G. **Vagrancy and Loitering**
    1. Two early offenses aimed at roaming around (vagrancy) with no visible means of support and standing around (loitering)
    2. Vagrancy and loitering have been tailored to meet modern problems of "bad public manners" of street people and gangs.
    3. **Vagrancy**—due process (void-for-vagueness) restricts power to criminalize vagrancy
        a. *Case: Papachristou v. City of Jacksonville (1972)*
    4. **Loitering**
        a. *Case: Kolender v. Lawson (1983)*
    5. Vagrancy and loitering can overcome the vagueness objection if they're defined to include more than just roaming around or standing around.
    6. San Francisco's efforts to legislate against these quality-of-life crimes
        a. *Case: Joyce v. City and County of San Francisco*
H. **Panhandling**
    1. Panhandling statutes call the ancient crime of public begging into service to control "aggressive" begging by "street people."
    2. Bans on panhandling don't apply to "organized charities" (Salvation Army).
    3. Panhandling is "speech" protected by the First Amendment.
        a. Right to panhandle is "commercial speech," and so it's less protected than other types of speech.
        b. States can control time, place (subways), and manner ("aggressive") of panhandling.
        c. States have limited ability control the content of panhandling (the right to ask for money).
    4. *Case: Gresham v. Peterson*
I. **Gang Activity**
    1. "Bands of loitering youth" scare ordinary people.
    2. Civil remedies, such as having injunctions to abate public nuisances, have been used to control gangs.
    3. *Case: People v. Acuna*
    4. *Case: City of Chicago v. Morales*
    5. Anti-gang ordinances raise due process questions (liberty and void-for-vagueness).
    6. Anti-gang ordinances meet due process and liberty requirements if they define loitering more specifically than "hanging out with no apparent purpose" (permissible to ban loitering "for the purpose of committing a crime").

III. Victimless crimes are a controversial topic.
- A. Applies only to adults—refers to crimes committed by adults who don't see themselves as victims
- B. **Victimless crime controversy**
    1. Referring to these crimes as "victimless" is controversial and involves the debate over the proper relationship between law and morality.
    2. The Wolfendon Report in 1950s England recommended decriminalizing private sexual conduct between consenting adults (homosexuality and prostitution).
- C. **Prostitution and Solicitation**—today, both patrons and prostitutes (male or female) commit prostitution, and it is a crime almost everywhere in the U.S.

CHAPTER SUMMARY

Issues of public order include both individual disorderly conduct crimes, such as fighting or making unreasonable noise, and group disorderly conduct crimes, such as unlawful assembly, rout, and riot. Public order crimes also include "bad manner" crimes known as quality-of-life crimes. These ancient crimes, such as vagrancy and loitering, have been applied to new situations like street gangs. Public order crimes highlight the tension between order and liberty and include the controversial category of "victimless" crimes, such as prostitution and solicitation.

The Model Penal Code was very influential in shaping the current law. The code limits conduct that qualifies as disorderly conduct *actus reus* to three kinds: 1) fighting in public; 2) making unreasonable noise or using abusive language; and 3) creating a "hazardous or physically offensive condition" like strewing garbage, setting off "stink bombs," or turning off lights in crowded public places. The code was also unusual in that it had a *mens rea* element.

In practice, the most common use of disorderly conduct laws is against fighting in public. Fighting can cause two harms: disturbing community peace and disturbing or endangering innocent bystanders.

Group disorderly conduct consisted of three misdemeanors at the common law: unlawful assembly, rout, and riot. All three were aimed at preventing the ultimate evil of open disorder and breach of the public peace. Unlawful assembly was committed when a group of at least three persons joined together for the purpose of committing an unlawful act. If the group of three or more started toward achieving their purpose, they committed the crime of rout. If the group actually committed an unlawful violent act, or performed a lawful act in a "violent or tumultuous manner," they committed the crime of riot (if there were twelve of them). Committing riot didn't require the group to plan their unlawful violent act in advance. It was enough that once together they came up with the plan of violence.

Some disorderly conduct crimes are now called quality-of-life crimes, but they're still aimed at the same conduct—"bad manners" in public places. Efforts to control bad manners in public underscore the tension between order and liberty in constitutional democracies. Order is acting in accordance with ordinary standards of good manners and decency. Liberty is freedom to come and go and do as we like without government interference. The U.S. Supreme Court has used the term "ordered liberty" to describe this need for both.

Quality-of-life crimes are minor offenses, but the broken-windows theory claims (based on mixed empirical results) they're linked to serious crime. In the 1980s, two scholars noted a deep public need for what they called a lost sense of public "good manners," especially in our largest cities. Professors James Q. Wilson and George L. Kelling (1982) suggested that what were labeled "petty crimes" weren't just "bothering" law-abiding people; they were connected to serious crime. They called this connection between disorderly conduct and serious crime the broken-windows theory. According to Kelling, research conducted since the article was written in 1982 has demonstrated a direct link between public disorder and crime. Others argue that both disorder and serious crime are caused by the same factors and that disorder does not always lead to serious crime.

There is widespread public support among all classes, races, and communities for controlling the offensive behaviors of "street people" and "street gangs." Most people are more worried about bad public manners (loitering, panhandling, public drunkenness, and prostitution) than they are about serious crimes (rape, robbery, burglary, and assault).

A number of state and city governments have passed criminal laws to regulate gang behavior. In some places, it's a crime to participate in a gang. Some statutes and ordinances have stiffened the penalties for crimes committed by gang members. Others make it a crime to encourage minors to participate in gangs. Some have applied organized crime statutes to gangs. A few have punished parents for their children's gang activities. Cities have also passed ordinances banning gang members from certain public places, particularly city parks.

Laws against loitering, vagrancy, panhandling, and non-criminal gang activity raise serious issues of due process (void-for-vagueness) and violation of First Amendment rights. Many loitering, vagrancy, panhandling, and anti-gang laws have been found to be unconstitutional. However, carefully written laws that are specific and content-neutral about time, place, and manner restrictions can be constitutional if other outlets for expression are available.

Government ability to regulate speech, including panhandling, varies with the type of public property involved. In traditional public forums, government power is weakest. Traditional public forums include public parks and streets. Government power is at an intermediate level in designated public forums—public places that the government has set aside or designated for speech activities. Auditoriums or public bulletin boards would be examples. Government power is strongest in nonpublic forums such as government office buildings and military bases.

In addition to criminal penalties, cities have also turned to civil remedies to control gang activity. For example, in the ancient civil remedy injunction to abate public nuisances, which is still used, government attorneys ask courts to declare gang activities and gang members public nuisances and to issue injunctions (court orders) to abate (stop) the public nuisance.

There is inherent conflict between the societal values of freedom or liberty, on the one hand, and order and security on the other. Both cannot be maximized at the same time. The problem is trying to strike a balance between the two. The U.S. Supreme Court uses the term "ordered liberty" to reflect the need for accommodation of both. This is also reflected in the debate between Stephen and Mill over the proper relationship of law to morality. Those who favor individual liberty (such as Mill) disapprove of using law to enforce morality. Those who feel that morality is important for keeping society together (Stephen) approve of using law to enforce morality.

"Victimless" crimes (the ancient "crimes against public morals") are a controversial issue. It pits those who believe the criminal law should enforce morality against those who believe the private, nonviolent, consensual behavior of competent adults is none of the law's business. The Wolfendon Report, a British report from the 1950s, recommended that private consensual adult homosexuality and prostitution be decriminalized.

Victimless crimes include crimes between consenting adults, and/or crimes in which the victim does not perceive themselves as being a victim. A number of types of offenses have been termed victimless. Among these are substance abuse, internet censorship, loitering, prostitution, sodomy, seatbelt law violations, helmet law violations, bans on bungee jumping, and laws against assisted suicide. Crimes involving a willing buyer and seller, such as prostitution, drug, and firearms crimes can also be victimless crimes.

Prostitution is an ancient business, prospering in all cultures at all times, in spite of being illegal. It's also a crime nearly everywhere in the United States. Prostitution used to be reserved for the act of selling sexual intercourse for money—and only selling, not buying, sex was included. Now, it means all contacts and penetrations as long as they're done with the intent to gratify sexual appetite. Both patrons (buyers) and prostitutes (sellers) can commit prostitution. In the past, the law recognized only women as prostitutes. Now both men and women who sell sex are prostitutes.

It's a crime not only to buy and sell sex, but also to solicit prostitution (sometimes called promoting prostitution, "pimping," or "pandering"). Soliciting prostitution means getting customers for prostitutes and/or providing a place for prostitutes and customers to engage in sex for money. Prostitution and promoting prostitution are misdemeanors in most states, but it's a serious felony when circumstances such as minors and violence are involved.

PRACTICE TEST BANK

MULTIPLE CHOICE

1. The _____ theory suggests that public order crime should be policed aggressively because it eventually triggers increases in more serious crimes, and therefore, stopping public order crimes is important in protecting the quality of life in a community.

    a. shattered dreams
    b. un-mended fences
    c. broken-windows
    d. cracked sidewalks

2. Crimes against morals and public order are termed _____ crimes.

    a. public disturbance
    b. breach of the peace
    c. public life
    d. quality-of-life

3. Broken-windows theory was formulated by _____.

    a. Boyce and Hart
    b. Wilson and Kelling
    c. LaFave and Scott
    d. Fulbright and Jaworski

4. Starting in the 1960s, courts began striking down vagrancy laws because they violated the _____ doctrine.

    a. cruel and unusual punishment
    b. void-for-vagueness
    c. *ex post facto* law
    d. *res ipsa loquitur*

5. One of the First Amendment requirements for a valid time, place, and manner regulation is that the regulation _____.

    a. be content-neutral
    b. serve any type of government interest
    c. be limited to places that are nonpublic forums
    d. apply only to symbolic speech

6. The term "panhandling" means _____.

    a. threatening others
    b. aggressive marketing
    c. begging
    d. stealing housewares

7. Because begging is clearly speech, attempts to regulate it must meet the requirements of the _____ Amendment.

    a. First
    b. Fourth
    c. Fifth
    d. Eighth

8. In attempting to deal with gang problems, many cities have utilized the civil remedy of an injunction to abate _____.

    a. public order crimes
    b. public nuisances
    c. quality-of-life crimes
    d. breaches of the peace

9. In contrast to the broken-windows theory, Skogan suggests that disorder (public order crime) _____.

    a. and more serious crime are not related in any way
    b. and more serious crime may both be caused by some other factor
    c. is caused by serious crime
    d. causes more serious crime

10. One of the reasons the 7th Circuit Court of Appeals upheld the anti-panhandling ordinance in *Gresham v. Peterson* was because the ordinance _____.

    a. met the standards of the rational basis test
    b. banned panhandling totally at all times and places
    c. banned panhandling only where the other person was touched by the panhandler
    d. did not ban panhandling at all times and places

11. In *Morales v. Chicago*, the U.S. Supreme Court held that the city's anti-gang ordinance was unconstitutional because it _____.

    a. violated equal protection in that it discriminated against gang members
    b. discriminated against young people in violation of equal protection
    c. was unconstitutionally vague
    d. was an unreasonable interference with First Amendment rights

12. The expression 'reading the riot act' comes from the British Riot Act of _____.

    a. 1615
    b. 1714
    c. 1813
    d. 1912

13. The crime of vagrancy refers to _____.

    a. persons standing around with no obvious purpose
    b. being poor and being seen in public
    c. being homeless
    d. poor people roaming around with no visible means of support

14. The crime of loitering refers to _____.

    a. being without any visible means of support or employment
    b. being homeless
    c. remaining in one place with no apparent purpose
    d. panhandling

15. Traditional vagrancy and loitering statutes were struck down by the U.S. Supreme Court because such statutes violated the _____.

    a. void-for-vagueness doctrine
    b. First Amendment
    c. right of interstate travel
    d. Eighth Amendment

16. Under the First Amendment, panhandling is deemed to be _____ speech, which gets only a low level of protection.

    a. symbolic
    b. political
    c. expressive
    d. commercial

17. A civil approach to attacking the gang problem involves an _____ to abate public nuisances.

    a. interlocutory decree
    b. injunction
    c. invective
    d. infraction

18. The term "victimless crime" typically only applies to behavior by _____.

    a. the poor
    b. minors
    c. adults
    d. gang members

19. In Britain, in the 1950s, the _____ Report recommended decriminalizing prostitution and consensual homosexual behavior.

    a. Whittendon
    b. Whittington
    c. Wolverton
    d. Wolfendon

20. Most modern prostitution laws _____.

    a. cover both the buyer and seller
    b. are limited to selling sexual penetrations
    c. are felonies for the first offense
    d. apply only when a minor is involved

21. Today's disorderly conduct statutes grew out of the common-law crime of _____.

    a. disturbing the public peace
    b. breach of the peace
    c. public indecency
    d. public disorder

22. The Model Penal Code approach to disorderly conduct differs from prior approaches in that the code includes _____.

    a. an *actus reus* element
    b. felony punishment
    c. a *mens rea* element
    d. starting a riot

23. At common law, the offense of unlawful assembly involved ____ or more persons joined together for the purpose of committing an unlawful act.

    a. two
    b. three
    c. four
    d. five

24. At common law, if the people committing an unlawful assembly starting moving toward achieving an illegal purpose the offense became a _____.

    a. riot
    b. rout
    c. unlawful gathering
    d. unlawful congregation

25. Under the British Riot Act of 1714, the felony offense of riot required participation of _____ or more persons.

    a. three
    b. six
    c. nine
    d. twelve

26. Government power to regulate speech and soliciting is weakest in public streets and parks which are known as _____.

    a. nonpublic forums
    b. forums by designation
    c. traditional public forums
    d. free speech zones

27. The debate between Stephen and Mill concerns the propriety of using the law to _____.

    a. enforce morality
    b. change society
    c. end discrimination against the poor
    d. protect children

28. In any society, there is a tension between _____.

    a. liberty and freedom
    b. order and stability
    c. license and promiscuity
    d. liberty and order

29. A pimp would be guilty of the crime of _____.

    a. pimpery
    b. promoting prostitution
    c. public indecency
    d. public obscenity

30. Conduct that conveys a message is called symbolic speech or _____.

    a. expressive conduct
    b. expressive symbolism
    c. communicative behavior
    d. symbolic behavior

TRUE/FALSE

1. Public order and decency crimes are relatively new offenses.
    a. true
    b. false

2. Order and liberty are values that can be in conflict.
    a. true
    b. false

3. The broken-windows theory was originally formulated by Stephen and Mill.
    a. true
    b. false

4. Many vagrancy and loitering laws were struck down under the due process theory of void-for-vagueness.
    a. true
    b. false

5. Loitering means to remain in one place with no apparent purpose.
    a. true
    b. false

6. At one time, all states had laws against vagrancy and loitering.
    a. true
    b. false

7. One of the reasons why enforcing laws against quality-of-life crimes is controversial is because it seems to target the poorest and weakest members of the community.
    a. true
    b. false

8. The Model Penal Code does not contain any disorderly conduct or breach of the peace crimes.
    a. true
    b. false

9. Quality-of-life crimes were enacted primarily in cities rather than in the country.
   a. true
   b. false

10. The Wolfendon Report recommended that prostitution not be decriminalized.
    a. true
    b. true

11. Crimes against public order and morals are sometimes referred to as quality-of-life crimes.
    a. true
    b. false

12. The term "panhandling" means begging.
    a. true
    b. false

13. Among the various types of forums, First Amendment rights are strongest in nonpublic forums.
    a. true
    b. false

14. Expressive conduct is not protected by the First Amendment.
    a. true
    b. false

15. Commercial speech is not protected by the First Amendment.
    a. true
    b. false

16. To be constitutional, time, place, and manner regulations must apply everywhere in the city or state.
    a. true
    b. false

17. To be constitutional, time, place, and manner regulations must not be based on the content of the speech.
    a. true
    b. false

18. A preliminary injunction is a temporary court order designed to freeze the status quo pending a full trial.
    a. true
    b. false

Study Guide

19. As compared to traditional disorderly conduct statutes, the Model Penal Code provision on disorderly conduct is unusual in that it has a *mens rea* element.
    a. true
    b. false

20. Under old English law, an unlawful assembly consisted of at least three people.
    a. true
    b. false

21. Under old English law, those who participated in an unlawful assembly could later be guilty of the offense of rout if they started toward achieving their unlawful goal.
    a. true
    b. false

22. Under the English Riot Act of 1714, it took at least ten people to form a riot.
    a. true
    b. false

23. The U.S. Supreme Court has never struck down a vagrancy or loitering law.
    a. true
    b. false

24. San Francisco was a city that enforced quality-of-life crimes against street people.
    a. true
    b. false

25. Victimless crimes always involve minors.
    a. true
    b. false

FILL-IN-THE-BLANK

1. First Amendment rights are strongest in _____ forums.

2. As compared to other forums, First Amendment rights are weakest in _____ forums.

3. Of the three types of forums, First Amendment rights have intermediate strength in _____ forums.

4. Panhandling is _____ speech.

5. To be valid under the First Amendment, time, place, and manner restrictions must serve _____ government interests.

210

6. The _____ theory suggests that tolerance of minor offenses can lead to more serious crimes.

7. The government can place _____, _____, and _____ restrictions on speech in public places.

8. A/n _____ is a court order to do or stop doing something.

9. _____ is remaining in one place with no apparent purpose.

10. Streets, sidewalks, and public parks are termed _____ forums.

11. The U.S. Supreme Court's term, ordered _____, reflects the need to balance the values of freedom and order.

12. Public _____ law provides a civil remedy for many quality of life problems.

13. In *Chicago v. Morales*, the U.S. Supreme Court invalidated a loitering ordinance aimed at _____.

14. Loitering and vagrancy laws were frequently found unconstitutional under the _____ _____ doctrine.

15. Nonverbal expression is also called _____ conduct.

ESSAY

1. Discuss the research regarding the link between social disorder and serious crimes. Explain the broken-windows theory and provide examples.

2. Compare and contrast individual disorderly conduct and group disorderly conduct. Give examples.

Study Guide

3. What is the void-for-vagueness doctrine and what impact did it have on traditional loitering and vagrancy laws?

4. Discuss the types of restrictions that the government can place on panhandling. Compare and contrast the three types of First Amendment forums.

5. Discuss the main points of the controversy regarding "victimless" crimes.

CHAPTER 12 ANSWER KEY

Multiple Choice

1. c	2. d	3. b	4. b	5. a
6. c	7. a	8. b	9. b	10. d
11. c	12. b	13. d	14. c	15. a
16. d	17. b	18. c	19. d	20. a
21. b	22. c	23. b	24. b	25. d
26. c	27. a	28. d	29. b	30. d

True/False

1. T	2. T	3. F	4. T	5. T
6. T	7. T	8. F	9. T	10. F
11. T	12. T	13. F	14. F	15. F
16. F	17. T	18. T	19. T	20. T
21. T	22. F	23. F	24. T	25. F

Fill-in-the-Blank

1. traditional public
2. nonpublic
3. designated public
4. commercial
5. significant
6. broken-windows
7. time, manner, place
8. injunction
9. Loitering
10. traditional public
11. liberty
12. injunction
13. street gangs
14. void-for-vagueness
15. expressive

CHAPTER 13
CRIMES AGAINST THE STATE

LEARNING OBJECTIVES

After studying this chapter, students will understand that:

- This chapter is about applying the enduring idea of balancing security and freedom during wartime emergencies.

- Treason is a fundamental weapon against *present* allegiance and support to foreign enemies.

- Crimes against *potential* terrorist attacks are subject to the limits placed on traditional criminal law.

- The most commonly prosecuted crime against the state since September 11, 2001, is "providing material support or resources" to terrorists or terrorist organizations.

KEY TERMS AND CONTENT

- **USA Patriot Act**—act passed by Congress following September 11, 2001, creating some new (and enhancing the penalties for existing) crimes of domestic and international terrorism; p. 438

- **treason**—crime of levying war against the United States or of giving aid and comfort to its enemies; p. 438

- **adherence to the enemy (in treason)**—breaking allegiance to your own country; p. 439

- **sedition**—the crime of "stirring up" treason by words; p. 442

- **seditious speech**—"stirring up" treason by means of the spoken word; p. 442

- **seditious libel**—writings aimed at "stirring up" treason; p. 442

- **seditious conspiracy**—agreement to "stir up" treason; p. 442

- **Smith Act of 1940**—U.S. statute aimed at Communists who advocated the violent overthrow of the government; p. 443

- **sabotage**—damaging or destroying property for the purpose of hindering preparations for war and national defense during national emergencies; p. 443

- **espionage**—the crime of spying for the enemy; p. 444

- **terrorism**—in the nonlegal sense, it means the use of violence and intimidation in the pursuit of political aims; p. 445

- **Anti-Terrorism and Effective Death Penalty Act (AEDPA)**—law defining new crimes of domestic terrorism and increasing the penalties for domestic terrorism crimes; p. 445

- **international terrorism**—terrorist acts dangerous to U.S. citizens committed outside the United States; p. 445

- **domestic terrorism**—terrorist crimes committed inside the United States; p. 446

- **weapons of mass destruction**—any destructive device used to commit acts of terror; p. 446

- **destructive device (in terrorist crimes)**—device used to commit terrorist acts (for example, bombs, poison gas, etc.); p. 446

- **conduct transcending national boundaries (in terrorist crimes)**—element in new antiterrorism crime statute that cites acts of terrorism that take place partly outside and partly inside the United States; p. 446

- **material support (in terrorist crimes)**—element in terrorist crimes that consists of helping terrorists or terrorist organizations; p. 448

- **proximity crimes**—ban conduct because of its closeness to other crimes; p. 448

CHAPTER OUTLINE

I. Treason
    A. Distrust of treason laws and the American revolution
        1. The only crime defined in the Constitution
    B. After the Revolution, the new government was fragile because it was new and needed time for loyalty and allegiance to take hold.
        1. England, Spain, France, and Native American nations threatened from all sides.
        2. Traitors, spies, and other disloyal individuals and groups threatened from within.
    C. Authors of the Constitution had mixed feelings about treason.
        1. They were tough on traitors who broke allegiance and were disloyal.
        2. Their own ancestors had fled from religious persecution and prosecution for treason.
        3. Treason was broadly defined in England to include thoughts and feelings that led to prosecution of innocent people.

4 Two concerns:
- a. Repression of peaceful opposition to government
- b. Conviction of the innocent because of perjury, passion, and/or insufficient evidence

D. Treason is defined in the body of the Constitution, where it's very difficult to change.

E. Elements of treason
1. *Actus reus*
   a. Levying war against the U.S.
   b. Giving aid and comfort to enemies of the U.S.
2. *Mens rea*
   a. Intent to give aid and comfort
   b. The purpose of betraying the U.S. by means of aid and comfort
3. Proof
   a. Two witnesses to *actus reus*
   b. Confession in open court

II. Sedition, Sabotage, and Espionage

A. **Sedition**
1. Ancient crime of "stirring up" treason (advocate violent overthrow of government) by:
   a. Speeches
   b. Writing (libel)
   c. Conspiracy
2. In the U.S. Code, sedition includes only advocating the violent overthrow of the government.
3. Smith Act of 1940
4. *Case: Dennis v. United States*

B. **Sabotage**
1. Damaging and/or destroying property related to war and defense material, buildings, and utilities (which includes transportation and harbors)
2. Producing defective property related to war and defense
3. Elements
   a. *Actus reus*
      (1) Destroy
      (2) Damage
      (3) Obstruct
      (4) Interfere
      (5) Contaminate
      (6) Produce defective war or national defense materials
   b. *Mens rea*
      (1) Purposely obstruct (or any other acts in *actus reus*)
      (2) Knowingly obstruct (or any other acts in *actus reus*)
      (3) Negligently obstruct (or any other acts in *actus reus*)
   c. Circumstance
      (1) At war
      (2) During national emergency

C. **Espionage (spying)**
   1. Definition of espionage—Secret intelligence gathering by spies about foreign people, activities, and enterprises for political and military uses.
   2. U.S. Code espionage elements (at any time)
      a. *Actus reus*
         (1) Communicate
         (2) Deliver
         (3) Transmit
         (4) Attempt to communicate, deliver, or transmit intelligence (information harmful to the U.S.)
      b. *Mens rea*
         (1) Purposely injure
         (2) Reason to believe use of intelligence will injure
      c. Circumstances
         (1) Intelligence provided to foreign government
         (2) Foreign faction or party
         (3) Foreign military or naval force
         (4) Foreign representative, officer, agent, employee, subject, or citizen
   3. U.S. Code espionage elements (during war)
      a. *Actus reus*
         (1) Collect any intelligence useful to the enemy
         (2) Publish it
         (3) Communicate it
         (4) Attempt to do so
      b. *Mens rea*—intent to communicate information to enemy
      c. Circumstance—time of war

III. Antiterrorism Crimes
  A. A number of relatively new statutes involve fighting terrorism.
    General crimes applicable to terrorist acts:
      1. Treason, sedition, sabotage, and espionage
      2. Murder, attempted murder, and conspiracy to murder also apply
  B. **The use of weapons of mass destruction**
     1. Elements
        a. *Actus reus*
           (1) Use
           (2) Threaten to use
           (3) Attempt or conspire to use
        b. *Mens rea*—without lawful authority (voluntarily)
        c. Circumstance(s)
           (1) Against a U.S. "national" outside the U.S.
           (2) Against any "person" inside the U.S.
           (3) Against any property inside or outside the U.S.

2. Definition of "weapon of mass destruction"
   a. "Any destructive device"—explosive, incendiary, poison gas, bomb, grenade, rocket, missile, mine, or similar device
   b. Any weapon intended to cause death or serious bodily injury by poisonous chemicals or precursors
   c. Any weapon involving a disease mechanism
   d. Any weapon designed to release radiation or radioactivity at levels harmful to human life

C. **Acts of terrorism transcending national boundaries**
   1. Definition—conduct occurring partly inside and partly outside the U.S.
   2. Types of conduct (*actus reus*)
      a. Commit violent crimes against any person inside the U.S.
      b. Create a substantial risk of serious bodily injury by destroying or damaging property within the U.S.
      c. Threatening, or attempting, or conspiring to commit (a) or (b)
   3. Circumstances
      a. Victims—U.S. government, members of uniformed services, officials, employees, and agents of the U.S.
      b. Property owned or leased by the U.S.
   4. Penalties
      a. Death for killing or death resulting from the act
      b. Up to life for kidnapping
      c. Up to 35 years for maiming
      d. Up to 30 years for assault
      e. Up to 25 years for damaging or destroying property

D. **Harboring or concealing terrorists**
   1. *Actus reus*—harboring or concealing persons who have committed or are about to commit a list of terrorist-related crimes
   2. *Mens rea*—knowing (or a reasonable person should have known) the crimes were going to be committed
   3. Penalty—fine and up to 10 years imprisonment

E. **Providing material support to terrorists and/or terrorist organizations**
   1. Prosecutions for violating Section 2339B are most frequent in practice.
   2. Material support crimes created after Oklahoma City bombing in the Anti-Terrorism and Effective Death Penalty Act (AEDPA) of 1996
   3. Amendment increased the AEDPA penalty in the USA Patriot Act (Uniting and Strengthening America by Providing Appropriate Tools to Intercept and Obstruct Terrorism) of 2001.
   4. The 300+-page Patriot Act is devoted mainly to criminal procedure—surveillance and intelligence, law enforcement information sharing, search and seizure, detention, and interrogation.
   5. Providing support to individuals or groups are proximity crimes because of their closeness to other crimes (44 other federal crimes) that terrorists might commit.

6. Material support to individual terrorists
   a. *Actus reus*
      (1) Provide material support to individual terrorist
      (2) Conceal or disguise nature, location, source, or ownership of material support or resources
   b. *Mens rea*—intending or knowing support or resources to be used in preparing or committing list of crimes helpful to terrorists
7. Material support to terrorist organizations
   a. *Actus reus*—provides material support or resources to terrorist organizations
   b. *Mens rea*—knowingly provides material support
   c. *Case: U.S. V. Lindh*
8. Most-argued issues in material support cases are constitutional.
   a. Due process—term "material support" is void-for-vagueness
      (1) *Case: Humanitarian Law Project v. Reno*
      (2) *Case: Humanitarian Law Project v. Gonzales*
   b. First Amendment—Providing material support violates right to free speech and association.

CHAPTER SUMMARY

To maintain themselves, governments everywhere have always had to rely on laws to protect them against foreign enemies and ensure the allegiance and loyalty of their citizens. During times of national emergency, we must try to strike the proper balance between security and freedom.

Treason is an ancient crime, and it is the only crime defined in the U.S. Constitution. Article III, provides: "Treason against the United States, shall consist only in levying War against them, or, in adhering to their Enemies, giving them Aid and Comfort. No Person shall be convicted of Treason unless on the Testimony of two Witnesses to the same overt Act, or on Confession in open Court." The treason sections in the U.S. Code flesh out these terms.

It is a crime against the state not only to commit treason but also to encourage others to overthrow the government by violence. Advocating the violent overthrow of the government is called sedition.

Sabotage is the crime of destroying or damaging property with the intent of interfering with and hindering preparations for war and defense during national emergencies. Espionage is another term for spying for the enemy. It includes gathering information harmful to national security and defense and communicating that information to hostile groups or nations.

Some of the recent legislation on these topics is part of the USA Patriot Act, which is the best known of the recent acts. It is an acronym for "Uniting and Strengthening America by Providing Appropriate Tools Required to Intercept and Obstruct Terrorism." Aimed at terrorists, it was passed and signed into law on October 16, 2001, after the devastating September 11th attacks on the World Trade Center and the Pentagon. The new laws divide terrorism into two kinds—international and domestic. Domestic terrorism involves acts within the U.S., while acts outside the U.S. are deemed international terrorism.

A number of sections of the U.S. Code are available for prosecuting crimes related to terrorists and terrorist organizations. Among the crimes specifically aimed at terrorism are U.S. Code Title 18, Chapter 113B, "Terrorism", the Anti-Terrorism and Effective Death Penalty Act (AEDPA) (1996), and the USA Patriot Act (2001).

Among the offenses in these new laws are: 1) the use of certain weapons of mass destruction; 2) harboring or concealing terrorists; 3) providing material support to terrorists; and 4) providing material support or resources to designated foreign terrorist organizations. The fourth-listed law has probably been the one most utilized by the government.

A number of legal challenges have been launched against these laws. The two most utilized challenges are due process (void-for vagueness) and First Amendment freedom of speech and association.

Chapter 13: Crimes Against the State

PRACTICE TEST BANK

MULTIPLE CHOICE

1. In response to the terrorist attacks of September 11, 2001, Congress passed the _____.

    a. AEDPA
    b. RICO Act
    c. Act to Prevent Terrorist Attacks
    d. USA Patriot Act

2. The crime of espionage involves _____.

    a. sabotage
    b. obstructing the war effort
    c. spying
    d. aiding or giving comfort to enemies of the government

3. Many anti-terrorism laws are included in the 1996 _____.

    a. International Terrorists Act
    b. USA Patriot Act
    c. Anti-terrorism and Effective Death Penalty Act
    d. Act for the Prevention of Terrorist Acts against the U.S.

4. The crime of _____ involves encouraging others to overthrow the government by violence.

    a. conduction
    b. sedition
    c. espionage
    d. treason

5. According to the U.S. Supreme Court in the Cramer case, _____ saboteurs is not treason.

    a. mere association with
    b. corresponding with
    c. aiding and abetting
    d. discussing politics

221

6. The crime of _____ involves damaging or destroying property to hinder preparation for war or national defense.

    a. treason
    b. espionage
    c. sedition
    d. sabotage

7. U.S. Code sections 2339A and 2339B of Title 18 make it a crime to provide _____ to terrorist organizations or terrorists.

    a. aid and assistance
    b. cover and concealment
    c. material support
    d. aid and comfort

8. The AEDPA was passed partly in response to the 1996 bombing of the _____ in Oklahoma City, Oklahoma.

    a. federal building
    b. U.S. arsenal
    c. Post Office
    d. airport

9. The offense of _____ is defined as levying war, adhering to enemies, or giving aid or comfort to the enemies of a nation.

    a. terrorism
    b. sedition
    d. espionage
    d. treason

10. One of the most famous American treason cases involved Julius and Ethel _____ who were executed for treason.

    a. Cramer
    b. Hess
    c. Alexander
    d. Rosenberg

11. The offense of _____ is the only one defined in the U.S. Constitution.

    a. espionage
    b. treason
    c. sabotage
    d. sedition

Chapter 13: Crimes Against the State

12. Terrorist acts committed in the U.S. are referred to as _____ terrorism.

    a. homeland
    b. internal
    c. domestic
    d. secondary

13. The most infamous domestic terrorist of recent years was _____.

    a. Karl Cramer
    b. Bernhard Goetz
    c. Timothy McVeigh
    d. George Siemens

14. The U.S. Constitution provides that a conviction of treason must be based on _____.

    a. a written confession or admission by a foreign government
    b. corroboration by physical evidence or testimony of three witnesses
    c. confession in open court or the testimony of two witnesses to an overt act
    d. proof beyond a reasonable doubt of remuneration from an enemy nation

15. Seditious speeches are termed seditious _____.

    a. conspiracy
    b. slander
    c. speech
    d. libel

16. The purpose element of the crime of treason is _____.

    a. to betray the U.S.
    b. remuneration
    c. revenge
    d. obtaining perquisites from foreign nations

17. As in *Dennis v. U.S.,* during the 1950s, the primary targets of federal sedition laws were the _____.

    a. Jehovah's Witnesses
    b. Nazis
    c. Communists
    d. Seventh Day Adventists

18. The two constitutional issues involved in the crime of providing material support to terrorists are _____.

    a. void-for-vagueness and First Amendment freedom of association
    b. *ex post facto* and bill of attainder
    c. Fifth and Eighth Amendment
    d. procedural and substantive due process

19. The crime of treason has _____ *mens rea* elements.

    a. two
    b. three
    c. four
    d. five

20. Weapons capable of killing numerous individuals by use of disease, poisons, and radioactivity are called weapons of _____.

    a. multiple homicide
    b. mass murder
    c. mass destruction
    d. multiple murder

21. Destruction and damaging are among the possible _____ elements of sabotage.

    a. *mens rea*
    b. circumstance
    c. *actus reus*
    d. concurrence

22. Treason is a _____ crime.

    a. strict liability
    b. vicarious liability
    c. specific-intent
    d. mandatory death penalty

23. The circumstance element of sabotage is _____.

    a. during war or national emergency
    b. while enemies are spying on the nation
    c. while the defendant is a citizen of the U.S.
    d. the information will aid the enemy in attacking the U.S.

24. Most of the USA Patriot Act deals with _____.

    a. sentences for terrorists, including expedited death penalty appeals
    b. creating new crimes
    c. punishing sedition
    d. procedural matters such as surveillance, search and seizure, etc.

25. The *mens rea* of providing material support to terrorist organizations is doing so _____.

    a. intentionally
    b. knowingly
    c. recklessly
    d. negligently

26. The U.S. Code separates spying into two separate crimes—_____.

    a. time of peace and time of war
    b. committed by U.S. citizen or non-citizen
    c. domestic or transnational
    d. overt and covert

27. The U.S. Constitution _____.

    a. leaves Congress free to create new definitions of treason
    b. leaves the courts free to create new crimes of treason
    c. prohibits the death penalty for treason
    d. limits the definition of treason

28. The current U.S. Code definition of sedition is limited to _____.

    a. seditious libel
    b. conspiracies that advocate violence against the government
    c. acts during actual time of war
    d. acts that are intended to aid enemies of the U.S.

29. The first sedition act in the U.S. was controversial because it included speech that _____.

    a. might be protected by the First Amendment
    b. encouraged young men to avoid fighting the French
    c. criticized the War of 1812
    d. advocated immediate, violent overthrow of the government

30. The federal Smith Act and *Dennis v. U.S.* (1951) involved laws against _____.

    a. espionage
    b. spying
    c. treason
    d. sedition

TRUE/FALSE

1. The primary aim of the USA Patriot Act is to fight international terrorism.
    a. true
    b. false

2. Sedition is the only crime defined in the U.S. Constitution.
    a. true
    b. false

3. Espionage consists of inciting others to violently overthrow the government.
    a. true
    b. false

4. Treason is an ancient crime.
    a. true
    b. false

5. Espionage means destroying government property.
    a. true
    b. false

6. Advocating the violent overthrow of the government is called treason.
    a. true
    b. false

7. Under U.S. law, espionage is only a crime during wartime.
    a. true
    b. false

8. In the U.S., treason can be punishable by death.
    a. true
    b. false

9. Under the U.S. Code, seditious conspiracy can be punishable by death.
    a. true
    b. false

10. The USA Patriot Act provides that it is a crime to conspire or attempt to provide material support to terrorist organizations or terrorists.
    a. true
    b. false

11. Sedition is a strict liability crime.
    a. true
    b. false

12. The U.S. Constitution specifies the type of proof required to convict of treason.
    a. true
    b. false

13. The right of peaceful association is protected by the Fourth Amendment.
    a. true
    b. false

14. The most commonly prosecuted crime against the U.S. since September 11, 2001, is harboring or concealing terrorists.
    a. true
    b. false

15. Timothy McVeigh was a domestic terrorist.
    a. true
    b. false

16. Julius and Ethel Rosenberg were executed for allegedly passing American atomic secrets to the Russians.
    a. true
    b. false

17. According to the U.S. Constitution, one of the ways treason may be proved is by confession in open court.
    a. true
    b. false

18. According to the U.S. Constitution, one of the ways treason may be proven is by the testimony of at least three witnesses to the same overt act.
    a. true
    b. false

19. The first U.S. sedition law was passed in 1917.
    a. true
    b. false

Study Guide

20. The first U.S. sedition law was limited to active advocacy of violent overthrow of the government.
    a. true
    b. false

21. In the 1700s, Britain had no laws against treason.
    a. true
    b. false

22. Murdering the president of the United States would be an act of sabotage.
    a. true
    b. false

23. The crime of espionage involves information.
    a. true
    b. false

24. Sabotage is a strict liability crime.
    a. true
    b. false

25. Espionage during time of war is a vicarious liability crime.
    a. true
    b. false

FILL-IN-THE-BLANK

1. _____ is the more common term for espionage.

2. _____ is advocating the violent overthrow of the government.

3. The U.S. Code prohibits providing _____ support to terrorists or terrorist organizations.

4. Destroying or damaging government property to interfere with national defense is called _____.

5. Making war or aiding those who make war on one's own country is called _____.

6. The USA _____ Act was passed quickly after the terrorist attacks of September 11, 2001.

7. _____ to the enemy means breaking allegiance to your own country and supporting an enemy country.

228

8. In *U.S. v. Lindh,* John Lindh tried to get the indictment against him dismissed on the ground that the material support provisions are _____.

9. Under recent legislation, implements of biological, chemical, or nuclear warfare are termed weapons of _____.

10. Under section 2339 of the U.S. Code, it is a crime to _____ or conceal terrorists.

11. The *mens rea* of providing material support to terrorist organizations is _____.

12. Damaging or destroying is the *actus reus* of the crime of _____.

13. Seditious writings are called seditious _____.

14. Laws prohibiting providing support for terrorist organizations may run afoul of the _____ Amendment's freedom of association.

15. The _____ doctrine may invalidate some anti-terrorism laws.

ESSAY

1. Compare and contrast sabotage and espionage. Be sure to provide examples.

2. Discuss, define, compare, and contrast treason and sedition. Be sure to provide examples.

3. What does the U.S. Constitution say about the crime of treason? Be sure to provide examples.

4. What are the two main Congressional Acts that deal with both domestic and international terrorism? Discuss some the things that are crimes under each.

5. What Constitutional challenges have been raised to the felony of providing material support to terrorists or terrorist organizations. How successful have those challenges been?

CHAPTER 13 ANSWER KEY

Multiple Choice

1. d	2. c	3. c	4. b	5. a
6. d	7. c	8. a	9. d	10. d
11. b	12. c	13. c	14. c	15. c
16. a	17. c	18. a	19. a	20. c
21. c	22. c	23. a	24. d	25. b
26. a	27. d	28. b	29. a	30. d

True/False

1. T	2. F	3. F	4. T	5. F
6. F	7. F	8. T	9. F	10. T
11. F	12. T	13. F	14. F	15. T
16. T	17. T	18. F	19. T	20. F
21. F	22. F	23. T	24. F	25. F

Fill-in-the-Blank

1. Spying
2. Sedition
3. material
4. sabotage
5. treason
6. Patriot
7. Adhering
8. void-for-vagueness
9. mass destruction
10. harbor
11. knowing
12. sabotage
13. libel
14. First
15. void-for-vagueness